horses

# HUNTER SEAT
# EQUITATION

# HUNTER SEAT EQUITATION

REVISED EDITION

## by *George H. Morris*

LINE DRAWINGS BY JAN CONANT
FOREWORD BY A. EUGENE CUNNINGHAM

DOUBLEDAY & COMPANY, INC.
GARDEN CITY, NEW YORK

Library of Congress Catalog Card Number 79–7071

This book is for all the people who, by buying the first edition, have asked for this new edition.

## My Gratitude

To Margaret Cabell Self, for putting me on a horse . . .
To V. Felicia Townsend, for giving me confidence . . .
To Otto Heuckeroth, who taught me about "The Horse" . . .
To Richard Watjen, for getting me to sit . . .
To Bertalan de Nemethy, who kept me on the right track despite the temptations and tangents offered by International Show jumping . . .
To Gunnar Anderson, who showed me how much can be done with a horse when properly ridden . . .
And most of all to Gordon Wright, who taught me to think about riding as a science and to love it as my art . . . and who still keeps teaching me how to learn.

*George H. Morris*

# Contents

PART 1 The Rider

## PART II Work on the Flat

# Contents

# List of Diagrams

# List of Illustrations

# *Foreword*

The scientific approach to the subject of riding is centuries old but still remains uncommon. Riding and jumping so captivate initiates that we are swept along as though caught by a current, swimming madly but making little or no effort to chart a course. When an exceptional individual gauges the current and plumbs the depths, most of us poor swimmers ignore his counsel and bounce merrily along from sand bars to deep water and, hopefully, back again.

My personal awareness of the value of counsel is the painful variety born of many years of near-total unawareness. No doubt many of you have also ridden and shown, as I did, by the proverbial "seat of the pants," without plan or organization, with no thought of hunter seat equitation as a subject for study and adaptation to our purpose. We do indeed get too soon old and too late smart.

Years of undisciplined riding make for keener appreciation of the text of this book, but the most fortunate are those who are able to read early in their riding careers, reread periodically, and apply constantly the guidelines set forth.

Reminiscing for a moment, I clearly remember a typically hot Fourth of July in the early 1950s at the late lamented Culpeper, Virginia, horse show, races, and riots. During an infrequent lull in the action I was introduced to a Mr. Morris from Connecticut and his young son George and later, out of their earshot, was told "that kid can ride." My informant, who shall go nameless, had been the source of much bad information and I was properly skeptical at the time, but time and events proved that the kid *could* ride. I next saw him during his student days at the University of Virginia. By then he had studied with General Humberto Mariles Cortes of Mexico and could be seen sifting techniques learned there. Shortly thereafter he became a member of the United States Equestrian Team and his many successes here and abroad from that time are well known.

Success as a rider in international jumping competition is the ultimate goal of most horsemen, but for George Morris it served as one more block in the carefully laid foundation of a career in teaching. This career, though brief in point of years, has been such an outstanding one that this book, detailing his methods and, hopefully, transmitting his enthusiasm, seems long overdue.

Much more than riding ability and experience are necessary in order to teach effectively. As in most fields, he is most apt to succeed who best loves his work. I count George Morris one of the luckiest men of my acquaintance, for through hours, weeks, and months of ceaseless teaching and riding, he loves every minute of it!

This enjoyment will, I believe, become obvious to you as the text unfolds the infinite care he has taken to relate his varied experience and knowledge to the clear refinement of his favorite, current, constant topic—hunter seat equitation.

                                    A. EUGENE CUNNINGHAM

*Warrenton, Virginia*

# Introduction

My intention in writing this book has been to put down on paper a systematic, practical method of learning to ride the hunter seat for the benefit of those riders who wish to do so. This particular system has been applied in practice by me and my pupils with considerable success, and thus I am convinced that it works, when correctly employed. As a matter of fact, I believe that it incorporates solutions to the vast majority of problems that beset the vast majority of riders and horses in training.

The methods outlined on the following pages are personal ones, drawn from a variety of sources, which have taken some years to put together in their present form. They represent the most effective methods I have been able to discover, and I am frank to admit that most of them are "begged, borrowed, or stolen" rather than invented. But though I have sorted out the various techniques I have seen and tried on the basis of what worked best in practice, my basic approach has proved to be quite classical.

"Classical" means begin with a classic seat. In my view, such a seat must be a versatile one, one which can enable a rider to have a comfortable hack through the country, go fox-hunting, show a hunter, or ride in a hunter seat equitation class, a dressage test (with a longer stirrup), or an open jumper class (with a shorter stirrup). With this seat, the rider should be safe, secure, have good style, and—most important of all—be versatile. He should be able to ride any kind of horse, help his horse when necessary, and show him to his best advantage. Only through searching for this all-round style can a rider assure himself of complete riding enjoyment and have access to all the many aspects and varieties of the sport.

No doubt much of the material in this book will seem familiar to you—either through other books, your own riding lessons, or your own observation. Let me repeat that none of the positions, controls, or exercises that I discuss in this book did I invent myself. They are, rather, a sifting and sorting of what I've learned in the many years I've appreciated good style and its origins from watching successful participants and their working methods.

Books are often ridiculed as a means of teaching riding and this attitude has always mystified me. Regardless of the subject of study, books can effectively give you the benefit of someone else's experience. By taking advantage of another's knowledge through books as well as personal instruction, you can stimulate your learning abilities and more quickly consolidate your technical security.

Therefore I suggest you read. Perhaps you are a complete beginner or perhaps you are a show-ring rider in need of a bit more polish. You might even be an accomplished, professional instructor going stale for want of new ideas and approaches to old-hat subjects. No matter what your status, you really cannot go wrong in trying someone else's solution to a problem that bothers you. You will benefit whether the method succeeds or fails, and have seen for yourself how well or otherwise it works. And let's hope the reading and trying prove fun in the process, too!

# Introduction
## to the Second Edition

This book is not a new book. In fact it has been kept almost
wholly intact. Rather, I would say I've given my original *Hunter
Seat Equitation* a face-lift. Nothing is new; we simply ride and
teach better, faster, and more economically today. Basics are
basics, and I stand fast by the principles I was taught thirty
years ago simply because they work. New fads come and go, and,
as a rule, they are misinterpretations, faulty techniques, or man-
nered exaggerations of sound techniques. It is very irritating
when teachers alter the terminology of this system even by one
apparently insignificant word. For instance, when teaching position of hands: hands are not over and in front of the withers;
rather, hands are just over and slightly in front of the withers. A
crest release is a legitimate old horseman's technique—it just
went unnamed for many years. Its advantages are twofold: freedom for the horse and, if properly executed, support for the
rider's upper body. But one does not simply move up to the
crest of the horse's neck; one moves up, rests on, and presses into
the horse's crest. We advocate riding with the stirrup on the
ball of the rider's foot; not, as is often seen today, out on the
toe. Upper body angulation must be rigidly adhered to when
developing a novice, or remaking a rider whose basics are poor.
Otherwise the pupil will invariably be ahead or behind his horse

before too long. A shoulder-in is not a horse that is just bending his neck. A shoulder-in is a shoulder-in! I could go on and on. It is a question of understanding and dedicated thoroughness in following theory and practice; and that is where both teacher and pupil often do not measure up to what I consider top standard.

Now, as to what I have done to this book. Firstly, there are many new pictures of riders familiar to the current generation of readers. This should add interest for those who like to see what's going on in hunter seat equitation today. Secondly, certain accidental conflicts in different parts of the first edition (the stirrup iron, by the way, should hit at the bottom of the ankle bone, not way below or above it) have been fixed. And thirdly, while I've deleted very little, I've changed and added words, sentences, and paragraphs throughout the book. One must read carefully or possibly miss the boat, for these changes are often quite inconspicuous. In other words, while the principles and basics have stayed the same, we've elaborated on them, made them clearer and more specific, and made the finer points more graphic than they were before. My hope is to continue to be able to do that to this particular book from time to time. My original aim, to write a classic and current "how-to" hunter-seat book, is still the same. And updating simply will mean occasional face-lifts, not a new face!

PART ONE

# The Rider

# 1

# Position of the Rider

## MOUNTING AND DISMOUNTING

There are many ways to mount a horse. In fact, different mounting methods have been disputed at great length and with some heat in the "Letters" column of a popular horse journal. Many people have adopted unconventional methods of mounting because of limitations imposed by youth, lack of height, lack of strength, or physical handicaps. However, while unorthodox methods may prove satisfactory with one's own horse or a horse that is quiet, many of them present serious safety hazards with young, unpredictable horses or horses of a nervous disposition. The basic method that I advocate has proven to be both simple and, more important, safe, no matter what type of horse is involved.

The first step in mounting is to take the reins in the left hand and face the rear of the horse, placing the left hand on the crest of the neck. Be sure that the reins are even, and short enough to hold the horse straight. If the horse persists in turning toward you (as many do), you will have to shorten the outside (right) rein even more. Even while still on the ground, you can thus establish a considerable degree of control over the horse, and by facing the rear, you are in a position to watch the horse's actions and judge the time to mount and also to brace against him and prevent him from moving forward if necessary. I do not agree with those who advocate facing the front or the side of the horse when mounting. This position, I've found, diminishes the rider's strength and agility, often resulting in an unsuccessful attempt to mount or, worse yet, a loose horse.

The second step, now that ground position and control have been established, is to place the left foot in the stirrup, the toe pointed toward the girth. A sensitive horse will move forward if the toe is stuck into his ribs, for then it acts exactly as a leg aid. Many riders find it difficult to hold this toe-girth position; this is only a matter of practice, however, and the stirrup leather may be lengthened if necessary. The third step of the mounting process is to place the right hand on the cantle of the saddle. With the left hand on the crest of the neck and the right hand grasping the cantle, there is little chance of pulling even a loose saddle down toward the horse's middle, as most of the rider's pressure is down upon the saddle, rather than pulling to the side. Under no circumstances, however, should you grasp the saddle with both hands. Even with a tight girth, it will be very likely to slip. Now, the final step is to swing up and sink slowly and softly into the saddle, place your right foot in the stirrup, adjust both reins, and assume the basic riding position. I can't emphasize the word "sink" too strongly. There is a great difference to the horse between a rider who sinks down upon the horse's back and one who sits down. A "cold-backed" horse cannot stand rough contact with his back, nor can a nervous, high-strung animal. The weight of the seat is an aid, and like any aid it must be employed with care and discretion.

Now to dismount. There are two ways, stepping off and sliding off. Both methods require that the reins are first shifted to the left hand. In stepping off, only the right stirrup is dropped, and the left is used as a step when the rider dismounts; in sliding off, both stirrups are dropped and the rider slides down the horse's side. Personally, I prefer the latter method, as there is less chance of being dragged if the horse should shy or bolt since both feet are free of the stirrups before the rider swings his right leg over the horse's rump. As soon as the rider has dismounted, the stirrups should be run up and the reins brought forward over the horse's head. This again is a matter of both safety and common sense. A dangling stirrup may startle or annoy the horse, and it can easily catch upon doorways or projections, causing serious and unnecessary accidents. As for leading the horse with the reins over his head rather than around his neck, it is obvious that they then act as a halter shank and provide much more control and leverage should the horse misbehave.

The right way to do almost anything with horses is mainly a matter of using your natural intelligence in an uncomplicated manner, and this holds true also for the rider's basic mounted position. Simplicity and economy of movement are the goals of classical technique; the position of the rider upon the horse is the first fundamental. From the very first we must use the essential, necessary ingredients and pare away the extras!

STIRRUP LENGTH

Before examining the rider's position, it is absolutely imperative to understand the function of stirrups and their adjustment. In principle, the reason for having stirrups is to provide a restful brace and support. The word "restful" applies here both to horse and rider; for the rider, the stirrup acts as a support for the foot and relieves the seat, while for the horse it accepts the displacement of some of the rider's weight and relieves the animal's back.

It is also important to appreciate the relationship between the rider's security, the horse's freedom of movement, and the length of the stirrup. The longer the stirrup, the longer the rider's leg and deeper his seat, thus increasing a horse's burden when working at fast paces or over jumps. Shortening the stirrup, conversely, shortens the rider's leg and lightens his seat, making the rider less secure, but the horse freer to gallop and jump. Two widely differing equestrian activities exemplify the contrast between long and short stirrups—dressage (as practiced in the Spanish Riding School of Vienna) and flat racing. In dressage work, emphasis is placed on the rider's security and control; in race-riding the rider wants to interfere with his horse as little as possible and depends for security upon balance, not leg grip. Riding to hounds, hacking over uneven terrain, or showing a hunter require neither extreme, but rather a happy medium between the two; enough control must exist to insure prompt obedience, but there must also be enough freedom of movement for the horse to perform his tasks easily. A correctly balanced hunter seat is impossible without a stirrup length that is correct, i.e., long enough for security yet short enough for freedom. Nonetheless, it is easy to prove, by comparing the illustrated examples of riders riding at different lengths, how closely related all phases of equestrian sport actually are, the only real difference being the slightly varied balance demanded by each. A good horseman, I feel, simply has to adjust his leathers to the situation and he is ready to participate in any direction.

Unfortunately, many people ride too short or too long. It takes an experienced instructor's eye, or an astute riding feel, to recognize false leg characteristics, such as reaching for too-long stirrups or being perched up on too-short ones. Two rules of thumb for judging stirrup length are useful: Before mounting, you adjust the stirrup leather so that the finger tips reach the stirrup buckles when the bottom of the stirrup iron reaches to the armpit of the straightened arm. Alternatively, you may adjust the stirrups after mounting so that the stirrup, hanging free, hits just at the bottom of the ankle bone. Both these methods are a bit tentative and depend too much on variations among riders' builds. In any case, a fairly accurate, individual stirrup adjustment must be made before attempting to deal with the basic riding position.

### BASIC POSITION DEFINED

For convenience, the rider's body can be divided into four principal parts: the leg from the knee down; the base of support, which includes thigh and seat; the upper body, which means all parts of the body above the base; and the hands and arms. A rider is considered balanced when his legs, seat, upper body, hands and arms co-ordinate correctly and are in equilibrium. By dividing the body into these four parts, it is simpler to isolate and correct specific faults, as well as to explain more clearly their effect upon one another. Of course, each of these major elements has many components; the ball of the foot is important to the leg; the seat bones are a major consideration in connection with the base; the head and shoulders greatly affect the position and function of the upper body. Each of these components must be put in place to create a unified whole. Thus, the rider's basic position must be described in considerable detail.

Establishing the rider's basic position is like building a house. We begin with the foundation, the bottom of the structure, which is the leg. I ask my pupils when mounted to place the ball of the foot (not the toe, as this undermines security, giving the foot too little stirrup support) in the middle of the stirrup and push the heel down and in, just behind the girth. The greater leverage afforded by this foot placement permits more depression of the heel; the heel is then more flexible and acts as a more sensitive aid, as opposed to riding with feet "home" in the stirrups. "Home" is the term used to describe placement of the rider's foot all the way into the stirrup as far as the heel of the boot. I do not recommend "offset" stirrups (stirrup irons slanted in an upward and outward direction), which are artificial and tend to cause stiff ankles, but I do like the added grip offered through rubber stirrup pads. The stirrup leather, by the way, should be vertical, and the stirrup iron close to perpendicular to the girth, with the outside of the iron being ever so slightly in advance of the inside of the iron.

After placing the toe out just a shade, establish contact with the horse with the calf of the leg and inner knee bone. Be careful that the toe isn't forced out further than fifteen degrees or so, nor turned in toward the horse. Do not grip more with the knee than the calf or vice versa. Exaggerated calf contact acts as an aid, while too much pressure on the knee acts like a pivot and causes the lower leg to swing. The leg in the correct position serves as a brace to the body and acts just behind the girth where it can exert the most influence on the horse. Remember that if the heel is placed too far to the rear the upper body will topple forward, and if the heel slips forward the upper body will fall behind the leg.

Moving upward we come to the base of support, the thighs and seat. It is important for the thighs to lie flat, gripping no more tightly than the knee or calf. In other words, contact with the horse should be evenly distributed between calf, inner knee bone, and thigh. We call this an educated grip. The seat itself is placed in the forward part of the saddle, close to the pommel. The rider must make every effort to feel his seat bones glued to the saddle through heaviness and deepness of seat. The base of support is considered strong and secure when the thigh muscles are conditioned and tight and the weight of the seat, through flexibility and feeling, remains in complete harmony with the horse's movements at all times. The jostled rider is usually one who has not learned to follow movement loosely; he tends to be stiff and to resist the rhythm of the gaits. Riding without stirrups is the only sure way of establishing an independent base of support, as will be explained in detail later on.

The rider's upper body is completely dependent upon his base and leg. The trunk of the body should be carried erect with the shoulders relaxed and the chest opened. A slight arch should support the upper back, but care must be taken not to arch the lower back, as this will bring the seat out of the saddle. With the rider looking straight ahead, his line of vision parallel to the ground, the eyes and head should anticipate the line of movement. A common fault is to allow the head to jut forward in front of the body. This tendency, and, in fact, any manifestation of stiffness or artificiality, should be quickly erased and replaced by a completely natural, yet elegant, tall carriage. Two other commonly observed posture faults are the stiff, hollow "sway-back" and the sloppy, hunch-shouldered, rounded "roach-back." Both of these undermine the use of weight as an aid. In general, the upper body must be supported firmly enough to enable it to influence the horse's back and hind legs, yet be loose enough to follow his movements and acrobatics in action. This takes time and practice to develop. Think how few good, strong riders are considered form-riders—that is the challenge!

Next in line we come to hands and arms. "Elasticity" is the word most often associated with the hands and rightly so, since rigidity there is quickly reflected elsewhere in both horse and rider. Elasticity is best attained by keeping the rider's elbow level with the horse's mouth, not only for pace control but also for head-carriage adjustment. The hands are held too low if they fall below the line to the mouth, and hands are too high if they break the line above the mouth. Except for specific corrections of head carriage, these extremes in hand positions have no purpose and greatly endanger the flexibility of hands and arms. In actuality a horse with a high head carriage should be ridden with a slightly higher hand.

In keeping with the straight-line principle, the hands should be placed above and slightly in front of the withers, two or three inches apart with the thumbs just inside the vertical. Hands assume weak, passive characteristics when flattened to a horizontal position; they tend to become too hard and strong when held completely vertical. A happy medium of positioning the hand halfway between horizontal and vertical encourages a combination of strength and softness. Wrists, too, should be held as

straight as possible, neither twisted nor bent. Twisting or bending the wrist causes unnatural arm and elbow displacement, thus
producing the stiffness that always results from any kind of
forced, irregular body position. The most useful hand is the one
strong enough to control, yet relaxed enough to allow freedom;
as we have seen, a straight position of forearm, hand, and wrist
is the simplest method of achieving the useful hand.

Methods of holding the reins are optional, really a matter of
individual preference. Mine is to hold a single rein between the
thumb and index finger and the third and fourth finger, and in
the case of two reins, the snaffle and curb, I separate them by
the little finger. Holding the rein outside the fourth finger is also
popular, but it eliminates the advantage of having a double grip
on the reins. It is essential to keep the thumbs flat on the reins
and all fingers around them so they won't slip, remembering
that control over the horse's mouth is exercised by closing or relaxing the hand and arm, not by pulling, twisting the wrist, or
opening the fingers. If you open your fingers, not only will the
reins slip and often be lost, but broken fingers can even result!

Now that the rider's basic position has been defined, let us
consider how it can be adjusted to deal with variations in the
movements of the horse. There is a simple technique for this adjustment, which becomes not only habitual but fast, providing
timesaving dexterity. And to be able to re-establish position
quickly during an unforeseen emergency is useful, to say the
least.

BASIC POSITION ADJUSTED

There are several ways to form or regain a good riding position.
The exercise I recommend here is one of the most useful, serving to concentrate the weight in the rider's heels while at the
same time enabling him to link together his points of leg con-

tact, namely the calf, inner knee bone, and thigh. In the following example this "seat correction" is described as a specific exercise of minutes' or even seconds' duration, but with practice it becomes a momentary stance to regain any loss of position and stability. This stance is termed the "two-point contact."

Immediately after mounting, the rider rises in his stirrups, and drives his heels down and in just behind the girth, while keeping the calf of his leg against the horse. Depending upon both his own and his horse's conformation, he will then be able to feel how far down his calf contact with the horse's barrel extends. It is important for the rider to understand how his own conformation relates to that of his horse, for this relationship changes with each horse ridden. A good leg easily becomes a bad leg through mistaken points of contact. A tall rider on a narrow, slab-sided horse will have less length of calf contact than a short rider on a more wide-barreled animal. It is for the horse's rib cage to fill out the relaxed, correctly placed leg, and not for the rider to attempt unnaturally to establish contact by leg or knee grip.

Once this leg positioning has been established, the rider sinks down into the front of the saddle, keeping his back tall and straight. Sinking just behind the pommel differs considerably from sitting down toward the back of the saddle; sinking is softer and more gradual in its effect on both the horse's mental and physical well-being. As this sinking takes place, the rider must take extreme care not to let his leg position slip either forward or back. With beginners, the leg can often be seen to swing forward in front of the upper body as the rider returns to the saddle, thus defeating the whole purpose of establishing leg position by standing up in the stirrups.

Regardless of the rider's competence, during position adjustments of any kind, he should look straight ahead. Balance is easily retained when the eyes are up and is lost just as easily when the eyes drop down. Trying to look at one's body position while riding is like looking at the steering wheel, gas pedal, or brake while driving a car, and the same thing applies to the arc over a jump while on a horse. Adjustments should be made with the eyes focused ahead, the mind concentrating on various body controls.

## TWO- AND THREE-POINT CONTACT

A major factor in controlling a horse is the rider's influence on its balance and, in particular, on the displacement of weight from front to rear, and vice versa. The rider's body, combined with his activity of hands and legs, exerts a strong influence in determining the focal point of the horse's balance under working conditions. Since there are two different general frames within which a horse performs, extended and collected, it follows that the rider's weight distribution should be adjusted appropriately to each. In general when the rider moves with the motion of his horse, he is encouraging an extended action, directing balance toward the forehand (front half of the horse). On the other hand, when his position tends to shift the horse's balance toward the rear, the rider is considered behind the motion of his horse, that is, retarding the horse's natural forward motion. Under no conditions should a balanced forward seat be confused with a rider perched ahead of the movement.

In referring to these different positions of weight distribution, I use the terms "two-" and "three-point contact." Two-point contact lifts the rider's weight off the horse's back and puts it down into his heels and stirrups. The body, by leaning slightly forward, somewhat lightens the burden on the horse's back and allows the balance point to shift toward the forehand. At this moment, the two nominal points of contact between horse and rider are the rider's legs. Contact, and therefore weight or influence of the rider's seat are of minimal importance. For the sake of smoothness and agility, when working and jumping at fast paces, two-point contact is required, and this is the position used in racing, hunting, galloping cross-country, showing a hunter, and in hunter seat equitation. This position, though, is used on straight lines only—not for turning or just in front of an obstacle. Two-point contact, as we have already mentioned, is especially valuable as an exercise position, encouraging the rider to weight and depress his heels. A rider who is able to remain in his two-point contact at a walk, trot, and canter is well on his way not only to being balanced but also to achieving independence in the use of his hands, legs, and seat. When learning and practicing this position, it is best for the pupil to hold the mane with one hand while taking a proper bridge of his reins with the other hand. This gives added support and eliminates any hanging on the horse's mouth for balance.

Three-point contact, the position used for most riding situations at normal paces, is distinguished by contact between the horse and rider through the weight of the seat as well as both legs, hence, three points of contact. This contact can be broken down still further, whether it be predominantly a crotch, seatbone, or buttock relationship with the saddle. Actually, the three-point contact is made the strongest by incorporating the buttocks, a position putting the rider well behind his horse, which can be most advantageous during emergencies.

However, since we are dealing here with fundamentals, we must stress that the seat bones, not the buttocks, support the upper body most of the time. In order to feel his seat bones against the saddle, the rider must sit up straight or ever so slightly in front of the vertical, not behind it. The three-point contact position is customarily used for cantering and any other especially collected flat or jumping work. The need for extra drive or restraint beyond that available to the hands or legs alone calls for this three-point position. Most open jumper riders, for example, habitually use three-point contact, since their success depends upon collection for control and lightness of forehand and general strength and agility. Also, one would ride behind his horse when working with colts, balky horses, buckers, rearers, or bolters. In fact, any horse demonstrating a severe vice should be kept well in front of the rider's seat and legs. Another case in point requiring more body riding would be during the approach to a particularly difficult or spooky jump, one likely to cause a severe hesitation or refusal. Remember, though, that with the exception of these examples I feel most strongly that, for the horse's comfort and freedom and for the rider's comfort and smoothness, one should be inclined forward according to the speed and gait in balance with the horse's movement. Of course, the only two gaits in which a considerable degree of forward inclination is required would be the posting trot and the gallop; in all other paces an inclination just in front of the vertical is proper.

Though they sound difficult to execute, both of these balanced seats must be available at a moment's notice, even for a rider of moderate skill if he is to be able to function under any range of circumstances. In fact, I feel that any rider's scope is dangerously limited and static if he lacks ability to ride either in two- or three-point contact at will. All the situations that may arise in riding can be dealt with by using one position or the other, and equal attention must be given to both. This is why riding without stirrups, which develops three-point contact depth, can contribute so much to the development of a strong seat and independence of the rider's hands and legs. In short, when riding a course of jumps, be it a hunter, jumper, or equitation class, one always incorporates all three positions depending upon what one is doing at that moment: a galloping stance (two-point contact), a crotch seat (three-point contact), or a buttock seat (three-point contact).

UPPER BODY ANGULATION

Before going into upper body angulation at different gaits, I want to discuss the rider's back as a specific entity. First of all, the correct use of the back is a very subtle thing both to learn and to teach, much more so than, for instance, the rider's leg. The weight of the rider's trunk really co-ordinates and clarifies all of the aids. Therefore it is of major consequence that one has the best possible back position in order to function. Starting at the bottom, the seat, the rider must sit on his two "ridgey" seat bones, neither forcing his buttocks out to the rear nor tucking them under so that he sits on his spine or flab. Once this correct sitting position had been felt, understanding of the back is simple. Without being stiff it should be as straight and as tall as possible. Make sure that a shoulder or a hip does not collapse to the inside of a turn. Especially the lower back must be relaxed and supple, since that is the part that follows the horse at all the sitting gaits while the upper back should be carried and arched, yet never allowing this arch to push the buttocks too far to the rear.

Another common upper body problem is that of leading with the head and chin. This unsightly habit always starts from riding with the wrong half of the body, the top half, and not with the calves and other driving aids. A good corrective exercise is to get the rider to touch the back of his collar with the back of his neck. And now, with these points in mind, we're ready to go on and examine how the rider should co-ordinate his upper body at different gaits with increases and decreases of speed.

In order to maintain balance reliably, the rider must co-ordinate his center of gravity with that of the horse. In general, it suffices if the rider's center of gravity is directly over the horse's, but never ahead of it. As mentioned previously, the upper body may lean behind the horse's center of gravity, in order to instill forward drive or to restrain it. However, for real smoothness, fluidity, and "invisible control," one must stay with the motion of the horse, each body relating to the other.

In principle, the faster a horse moves, the farther forward his center of gravity shifts. The rider's body, then, must lean farther forward in proportion to the speed of the horse. It is this action, sometimes referred to as the "closing of the hip angle" or "upper body angulation," which enables the rider to be with the motion of his horse at all times. When the rider is behind the motion, his upper body remains erect, which places his center of gravity behind the horse's. If the rider closes his hip angle too much in relation to the horse's increase in speed, he will find that his center of gravity has moved ahead of his horse's, a position that drastically lessens control. Only a few especially talented riders are able to ride ahead of the motion and still keep the horse in balance.

An understanding of these angles of the upper body is absolutely necessary to smoothness, poise, and control when riding. It follows that each gait requires a somewhat different degree of forward inclination. When the horse is stationary, the center of gravity for both horse and rider is directly in the middle, halfway between head and tail, and the rider sits perfectly straight. When backing up, the weight of the horse shifts to the rear somewhat and the rider must follow this shift by remaining on the vertical—not falling forward. When the horse is walking, a similar shift forward occurs. Because of the slow speed of walking and backing, the alterations in the rider's center of gravity and degree of hip angulation are very small.

Sitting to the trot also creates a delicate shift forward, at most a forward inclination of a couple of degrees from the vertical, while posting to the trot requires a shift of perhaps twenty degrees in front of the vertical. It is at the posting trot that the difference between riding with the motion and riding behind the motion can be most clearly demonstrated. Any rider should be able to feel the distinctly different balance that is involved in posting straight up and down, in sitting on the buttocks (riding behind the motion), and in posting in a forward position on the thighs and crotch with the plane of ascent and descent inclined forward (riding with the motion). If the rider shifts his weight so far forward in rising to the trot that his weight exercises little or no influence on the horse, he is considered to be ahead of the motion, and this is right only for certain circumstances; namely, for a horse with a "cold" back or a sore back; or perhaps as an exercise for a rider who is habitually behind the motion.

During all sitting gaits we want to produce a rider with an elegant self-carriage yet one who is supple and deeply glued to the horse. These characteristics are not always easy to maintain, as it's often hard for people to learn to follow accurately the horse's movements with their seat and lower back. Whenever the seat bones are firmly riveted into the saddle, the shock must be absorbed by the almost imperceptible undulation of this lower portion of the rider's back. Often, this movement is consciously produced by the rider and consequently exaggerated and wrong. A good rule to follow is to allow the upper body to be carried as much as possible by the horse while the lower legs do the work by squeezing.

The posting position also implies the correct position for the hand gallop. The reason these two gaits require the same upper body angulation is to compensate for the rider's center of gravity (balance), which must shift forward a bit as he comes out of the saddle. The canter is a gait that involves collection, for a horse's weight to be distributed more toward his hocks, but the correct upper body position is the same as that for the sitting trot, a few degrees in front of the vertical.

In essence, the posting trot, the hand gallop, and basic jumping position are the same, and this makes it possible for the pupil to acquire a jumping seat while learning how to trot. Understanding and precise control of body angulation enable the rider to minimize the activity of his back and weight, a very positive asset in attaining smoothness both on the flat or over jumps. Thus, we generally associate riding with the motion with smooth cross-country, hunter, and hunter seat equitation, as the rider and horse must move as one in this work. The forward inclination of the rider's body in this position greatly relieves the horse's back over the long distances and while moving over uneven terrain; it is absolutely necessary for the horse who has a very sensitive, or "cold," back. When we are primarily concerned with maximum control and the greatest security, however, we find that these things are best achieved by riding behind the motion, with a deep, secure seat. To be sure, this usually involves a certain loss of grace, as the rider is always at work catching up to his horse, so to speak. However, when riding green horses or open jumpers, in dressage, or at any time when more collection is required, we will require more control, and therefore the deeper three-point seat. Thus it can be seen that solving the vast number of riding, hunting, or showing problems cannot be done with a fixed position of the upper body. Many people fear form-riding for this very reason, and they are right. Unless flexibility is stressed from the beginning of instruction and practiced dutifully, the rider will develop a single, mechanically stiff seat and be unable to adjust to new problems as they arise.

### RIDING WITHOUT STIRRUPS

The earlier part of this chapter has covered basic position and stressed how critically important it is for the rider's aids to function independently of his security in the saddle. Riding without stirrups is the most natural, efficient way for a rider to achieve this kind of independent security. It can provide him with a strong base of support and an independent control over hands and legs by teaching him to follow the horse's movement with the small of his back instead of tensing and stiffening against the different motions.

In riding without stirrups, it is better to pull the buckle down from the bar about eighteen inches before crossing the stirrups over the wither, making sure they are flat under the flap. The lump caused by leathers crossed any other way tends to prevent the rider from placing his leg normally. The rider's position should be exactly the same as if he were riding with stirrups. The foot should be held with the toes raised, as if in a stirrup, for the tightened calf muscles that result from the lowered heel are essential to the firmness of the leg position. Neither the legs nor the arms should be permitted to hang limply.

When riding without stirrups, the position should be corrected immediately whenever even a slight loss of position has occurred. Such adjustments will have to be repeated very frequently, especially at the beginning, and they will also be required at the end of every suppling exercise. To adjust or correct his basic position the rider grasps the pommel of the saddle with his inside hand and lowers his thighs and draws his seat forward toward the pommel while holding the legs in position. Also the pommel offers enormous security when one is learning to ride without stirrups. A general tendency is for the knees and thighs to ride up, forcing the seat bones and buttocks to the back of the saddle, something we most definitely want to prevent. By holding the pommel the rider is able to pull his crotch, thighs, and seat forward into the front part of the saddle, after which there is no place for the knees and lower legs to go but down. Of course the heel, not the toe, must be pulled down. Once the seat has been brought forward and glued into the saddle, and the legs lengthened into proper position, the rider has felt the correct way to sit even though artificially aided by holding the pommel. Remember that whenever this feeling has been lost a readjustment must be made. Later on, after considerable strengthening of the thighs and seat, we'll be able to re-establish the seat without resorting to the pommel at all.

All sorts of suppling exercises and calisthenics should be practiced while riding around the ring without stirrups at a walk or slow trot. The following ones are some of the best: one hand planted on the hip; one hand placed on the head; one hand behind the back; the arm extended, rotating in circles going forward, down, back, and up; one arm held straight while the body twists, the rider first touching the horse's ear, then reaching down and touching the toes, and then turning to touch the horse's tail. An exercise suitable for jumping preparation is to lean forward with the upper body going onto the knees and thighs. This is also good for balance, and one can do the same exercise in reverse, leaning back to almost touch the horse's rump with your head. Other exercises include: rolling the head, rotating the toes in a circle in and out and up and down, removing the calves from the horse's sides and bringing them back. Naturally, a little imagination will bring to mind many, many other exercises of a similar nature. Posting to the trot without stirrups will help to strengthen a loose, rounded thigh muscle. Indeed, almost any calisthenic done without reins or stirrups will aid a strong seat and independent balance.

The advantage of this kind of work without stirrups, with one hand bridging the reins, is that it can be practiced individually and thus is useful for group lessons. The ideal exercise, however, is to have no reins at all, as well as no stirrups, and this is possible only with individual work on a longe line.

LONGEING HORSE AND RIDER

Longeing is the ideal method for horse, rider, and teacher to work together to produce a first-class seat. With no stirrups or reins, the rider is compelled to rely completely upon balance and rhythm; hanging on to the horse's mouth is impossible and there is no supporting stirrup to facilitate leg grip. There is no doubt that this is the best way to learn to sit, but time and considerable individual attention are needed.

For progress and safety to be assured, thorough knowledge of longeing equipment and how to use it are needed. The gear consists of side reins, a longe whip, and the longe line. The side reins establish the horse's head carriage, the whip controls its pace and track on the circle, and the line restrains the horse from pulling out of the circle or going too fast.

Longeing is a simple task if prepared for and accomplished in this manner. First, attach the side reins below the regular rein from the bit ring to the girth. All longeing should be done with a regular plain snaffle, to encourage the horse to go to the bit and stay there. Longe the horse several times with loose side reins before shortening them for control. It is wise to make sure the horse longes quietly in both directions before asking the rider to mount, for horses unaccustomed to side reins occasionally resist and rear up, sometimes falling over backward. While longeing, the instructor should keep the rein in his inside hand (left hand when the horse circles to the left) and the whip in the opposite, outside hand. The horse should learn to stay on the circle at the desired pace without cutting in on the circle or pulling out, dogging along, or rushing on too fast. Once the pace and diameter of the circle have been established, the rider is ready to mount. The stirrups have of course been removed from the saddle, the reins have been knotted just in front of the withers so they do not loop down, and the side reins have been attached.

Once mounted, the rider places his outside hand on the pommel and his inside hand on the cantle. This rotates his shoulders slightly in the direction of movement, though there should be no conscious effort to twist the shoulders toward the inside. Holding the saddle with both hands in this manner, the pupil constantly pulls himself down and forward into the saddle, carrying his toes up. Once a measure of confidence and security has been established, the rider can remove both hands from the saddle and practice the exercises mentioned previously. Both hands and legs are now free, and the rider should be able to exercise his calisthenics at the walk, trot, and canter, both in the two- and three-point contact.

Basic position now having been covered in some detail, it's

time to put it to work. Riders too often are seen riding their position or posing on the horse's back, doing nothing at all about really riding the horse. Obviously this kind of riding is pointless and valueless for both horse and rider. What we are interested in is influencing the horse, "making him operate," and teaching him to do things. So in consideration of this aim, the next chapter will deal with our aids or controls, how they work and why, and the difference they make to horse and rider.

# 2

# The Rider's Aids

Aids are the rider's means of communication with a horse. Among themselves people communicate primarily through words; with horses they communicate primarily by the use of aids, either natural or artificial.

The natural aids are the rider's hands, legs, weight, and voice, in other words, elements of his own body. The use and refinement of these natural aids, often in conjunction with the artificial ones, make up the better part of a rider's struggle to gain real competence. And only through intelligent use of these aids can any horse be expected to perform his job satisfactorily. However, their independent and effective use depends a great deal upon the development of a correct position and seat. There are no short cuts.

In essence, the artificial aids are accents; they enforce and enlarge the natural aids. Sticks, spurs, martingales, bits, and auxiliary reins are good examples of what is meant by artificial aids. The stick, whip, or crop is the strongest of all the artificial aids, being the most painful and the loudest, and both pain and noise contribute to a horse's fear. Fear causes the horse to run forward and, therefore, the stick is used to evoke a forward response when other, milder, driving aids have failed. The spur produces pain, a sharp, pricking pain in the ribs. This pain is more intense than ordinary leg pressure and becomes an accent to the leg when more sensitivity from the horse is needed. Again the stick and spur are used as a follow-up to a leg that has failed to activate the horse sufficiently.

The various types of martingales mechanically influence the horse's head carriage in one way or another and prevent it from being too high or low. A wide variety of special bits and auxiliary reins are also used to combat head and mouth problems, each problem necessitating a different correction. The effective employment of artificial aids requires experience and above all moderation and common sense. Artificial aids can become the "knife in the monkey's hand." That is why we prefer the standing martingale, which acts on the bridge of a horse's nose, for all but advanced riders. Running martingales, German martingales, draw reins, chambons, etc., work on the sensitive bars of the horse's mouth and have no place in beginner or intermediate equitation.

### CLASHING OF AIDS

The conflict or clash of aids refers to the rider's making opposite requests at the same time, such as pushing and pulling. When asking for an increase of pace and simultaneously pulling in restraint, the rider is clashing his aids, which only confuses the horse. Only during collection, at an advanced stage of riding, do the aids appear to clash, but collection is actually not the result of clashing, but rather a sophisticated co-ordination of driving and restraining aids. Aids used in conflict with one another usually result from the rider's not having developed independence in his seat, confusion on his part, or simply a lack of knowledge.

Examples of this common fault are often seen in an inexperienced rider's going from a halt to a trot and then back to the halt. The hands remain tight and fixed on the horse's mouth while the legs drive forward to the faster gait, and when halting, the legs still grip tightly as the hands close to decrease pace to a stop. Examples of aids clashing are also commonly seen out hunting; the horse is driven over the jumps while rider's hands remain stationary, not releasing the animal's head and neck. During the schooling of green horses, one must be careful to isolate aids, using them independently and clearly, abandoning one aid before using the other.

Aids, both natural and artificial, can be segregated into two categories, driving and restraining. The driving aids are the leg, weight, voice, stick, and spur; restraint comes from the hand, weight, voice, and such accessories as auxiliary reins or martingales. The use of an aid from either category should cease before one from the other category is undertaken; otherwise, there will be a conflict of aids.

A horse manifests his reaction to a conflict of aids in two ways; he ignores one of the aids and sets up a defense against the other. Returning to the example of trotting and stopping, one of two reactions will result depending on whether the horse is keen or placid. The lazy horse will become sour or nappy and less inclined to go forward into the fixed hand. Becoming harder and harder to push, he thus ignores the driving aids that are compelling him toward the unyielding hand. A horse of this sort, unless corrected, easily becomes balky and rears. The keen horse, on the other hand, ignores the fixed hand, leans on the bit and becomes a puller. These are the so-called "hard-mouthed" horses, and they are more often that way because of a rider's mistake than through any fault of conformation. Through forever attempting to escape a leg grip, they become even more keen and tense, and often become runaways or nervous jiggers. These are defense mechanisms, and to avoid such problems initially, it is necessary for the rider to understand the co-ordination of aids, even as a rank beginner. The more slowly and more carefully a rider learns a sound sequence of aids, enabling him to produce a smooth increase or decrease of pace, the less likely he will be to produce a problem horse.

## CO-ORDINATION OF AIDS

Co-ordination of aids promotes proper training as quickly as conflict of aids destroys it. Any given movement required of a horse must usually be obtained through the combined effort of several different aids and an interaction of several parts of the rider's body. In order to move the horse from a halt to a walk, the leg pressure is increased, while the hands must relax their hold somewhat. The amount of pressure added by the legs must be matched by the amount of pressure relieved by the hands, and vice versa in stopping. The sequence is very similar to driving a stick-shift car—co-ordinating the clutch, gas, and brake; all three must work together, if a smooth ride is to result.

In commanding a horse to perform a certain exercise, the demand must be fully understood by the rider, and his aids co-ordinated in such a way that the horse is both directed and allowed to execute his task. For example, when backing a horse, the rider must know the proper sequence of backing commands that will elicit from the horse a predetermined number of backward steps. In other words, the rider must know, at least intellectually, how the exercise should be performed. He then combines his aids in a sequence that is slow and mechanical in the early stages of learning, but that becomes automatic later on. The correct sequence of co-ordinated aids for backing, for instance, would be as follows: First, the rider closes and fixes the hands, preventing the horse from walking forward; then he applies both legs actively just behind the girth, causing the horse to move up into the fixed hand; since at this point the hand blocks all forward escape from the active pressure of legs, the horse moves backward, and as he does so, the rider's upper body and weight come into play and he braces his back slightly in the direction of movement. This sequence becomes almost invisible, however, as the rider acquires finesse, a finesse that results from feeling the precise amount of hand, leg, and weight necessary to back quietly and smoothly.

Another good example of co-ordinating the aids is found in executing the circle. The co-ordination here is in a lateral direction, from side to side, rather than in a longitudinal direction backward and forward. As the inside hand takes up and increases pressure through the action of an indirect rein, the outside hand moves out and yields to the front in direct proportion to the inside hand's pressure. Thus, one hand complements the other so that the horse can bend into his turn. The legs co-ordinate in a similar way on a circle. The inside leg, placed just behind the girth, acts as a driving, bending force. The outside leg lies about a hand (four inches) behind the girth, where it acts as a supporting aid, controlling the haunches and keeping them on the track of the circle. These examples of using co-ordinated aids as means of eliciting specific movements set the pattern for all controls. The understanding of the aids in their isolated forms is important, but they are much more effective functionally when used in conjunction with one another.

OUTSIDE VERSUS INSIDE

In conjunction with the working layout, the rider should know what is meant by the "inside" versus the "outside," and this should be taught early. The terms are necessary to understand both in reference and in use of controls. Inside refers to the side nearest the center of the ring; outside to the side nearest the wall or edges of the ring. Horses, like dogs and people, do not travel in a completely straight line; they are a bit one-sided. The ultimate carriage for the riding horse is to be perfectly balanced and light in both directions, remaining straight. The natural crookedness to one side must be overcome, and this is corrected by specific exercises.

It is easy to learn to remember the difference between inside and outside even if one is not working in a ring, for there are other factors that take precedence over relation to the center of the ring, one being that the inside always corresponds to the side around which the horse is bent. Thus, for example, when the horse is moving around the ring to the right in the left shoulder-in, the inside of the horse and the inside influences are all on the left. This is true of any lateral work regardless of directional movement. The other precedent is concerned with counter-cantering work. Because the horse is always bent imperceptibly to the lead he is taking, the lead takes precedence over direction. Take for instance cantering to the left on the right lead. In this case the inside is the right. At the trot, it can be the diagonal, or shoulder, opposite to which the rider is posting.

In summary, in turns the inside is toward the center of the circle around which the horse is turning. On a straight line, the inside is always the same side as the lead on which the horse is cantering or opposite to the diagonal on which the rider is posting. In any bending work, it is on the side to which the horse is bent, which will also be the rider's inside influence. This is enough for the beginner to know.

### LATERAL VERSUS DIAGONAL AIDS

A useful concept for the rider to understand is that of lateral and diagonal aids, for the distinction can help to clarify the coordination of his aids in varied exercises. Lateral aids are those that act predominantly on the same side, i.e., the right hand and right leg. Diagonal aids are those that act predominantly on opposite sides, i.e, the left hand and the right leg. The predominant aid, whether lateral or diagonal, is usually supported on the opposite side, however. Both reins and both legs work together even though one or the other is the stronger.

A good example of lateral aids is found in the shoulder-in, a schooling exercise that encourages lateral flexibility in the horse. In the shoulder-in, though the horse's frame is considerably bent he travels in a straight line. To use the right shoulder-in as an exercise demonstrating lateral aids, the horse is bent by the right indirect rein and the right leg at the back edge of the girth. These two aids are the more active in relation to the left rein and leg even though the latter are supporting, holding, and correcting the horse most of the time. Thus the shoulder-in is considered to be effected by lateral aids.

In contrast, the haunches-in, another exercise concerned with lateral suppleness, demands for its execution diagonal aids. The haunches-in exercise also follows a straight track with the horse looking in the direction of movement, his hind quarters following a separate track to the inside, parallel with the track of the front feet. The horse is bent to the inside by the rider's inside indirect rein and around his inside leg, but it is the rider's outside leg that displaces the haunch, the more active aids being diagonal, the inside hand and outside leg.

## USE OF THE RIDER'S EYES

While the rider's eyes do not directly influence the horse and therefore cannot be considered aids, they nevertheless affect the aids, both consciously and unconsciously. First of all, the eyes contribute to the rider's balance, or lack of it, both on straight lines and on turns; if the eyes work correctly, the aids themselves tend to work more effectively and automatically. Unless the rider's eyes anticipate his direction of movement, his performances will lack continuity and suffer from late reflexes. An automobile driver utilizes his eyes in much the same way as the rider should, by following his path of direction and anticipating the movements that will be required in the immediate future. The driver looks into his turn, not at the steering wheel. So it is with a rider giving aids. When he turns his head in the new direction he anticipates taking, his body and weight shift, giving a subtle signal to the horse slightly in advance of the more direct aids to turn; the horse then becomes more responsive to the actual aids when given.

By the same token, if the rider drops his head to look down at his hands, or feet, or the horse's head, there is a subtle shift of weight that the horse will be aware of, but which will prove to mean nothing. Thus it is important to learn to see without looking, or, in other words, to use peripheral vision to watch your horse, reserving your direct glance exclusively for the direction in which you are about to go, whether this is straight ahead or turning. The rider must learn to ride by feeling, not by looking, and if he keeps looking down, he will never learn to feel. Feeling, like anything else, must be practiced, and the rider must develop the visual discipline to maintain his independence of eye, that is, to continue to look ahead while feeling what his own body is doing as well as his horse's.

In short, the eyes must impart directional quality and balance and should have little to do with the rest of the physical apparatus working below; they remain elevated, their job being outward and projecting, aiding the unification of horse and rider through feel, not examination.

## LEG AIDS

There are three basic placements of the leg in which it acts as an aid: at the girth, a hand's breadth behind the girth, and in front of the girth toward the shoulder. The back edge of the girth approximates the middle of the horse; and it is here that the whole horse is most affected by the legs, for this is where they have the maximum driving power for forward movement. Accordingly it is at the back edge of the girth that the inside leg remains most of the time, as it is necessary for this leg to constantly maintain a driving and bending influence. Riders who position their legs too far back or too far forward not only jeopardize their balance, but also greatly weaken their controls. The position just behind the back edge of the girth is the position of power.

As soon as the leg assumes the second position, that is, a hand's breadth behind the girth, it activates the horse in another way completely. Whereas the first leg position affects the horse as a whole, the leg in the second position controls only lateral displacement of the haunches, a sideways signal that has nothing to do with moving the horse forward or bending him like a bow. The rider's outside leg is ordinarily concerned with holding the haunches on a straight or circular track. Thus this leg, let me repeat, is normally placed a hand behind the girth, while the inside leg is at the girth. Each of these legs assumes its primary function, the inside one to drive and bend and the outside one to drive and hold straight. These two leg positions are all that the average rider need utilize, for the third placement forward is a bit risky and only necessary for advanced training.

This third position, in which the leg is brought forward of the girth and into the shoulder, is also questionable because it endangers balance. The leg so far forward of the upper body is apt to force the rider behind the motion, letting the preservation of his forward position become dependent on the horse's mouth. However, used against the shoulder of the horse by an experienced rider, this leg does exert a powerful control over such lateral work as exaggerated bendings or shoulder-ins on the circle. Here it is a very useful aid, working on the forehand in exactly the same way as the second leg position works on the haunches.

Only through mastery of these various leg positions, and understanding when to use which one, will the rider be able to execute the various advanced riding exercises which do so much to produce a softer horse, one who is easier to control and more reliable.

## HANDS—GOOD, BAD, "NO," EDUCATED

Good hands derive from a good seat, for they must be totally independent from the rest of the rider's body and the movements of the horse and be light and elastic. Good hands must be able to co-ordinate automatically for increasing and decreasing pace and employ the five basic rein aids so that they can bend, stop, and turn the horse at will while always maintaining sympathetic contact.

The obvious converse of good hands are bad hands. They substitute themselves for support as a foundation for the rider's upper body. To support balance in any degree with the hands is bad. Rough, severe, and cruel hands are an especially serious fault in a rider because of the very sensitive nature of the horse's mouth. Bad hands have no place in riding.

"No" hands, hands that have no feel of the horse's mouth at all, do have a useful place in riding, though they can be exaggerated to a fault. In some hack classes and at the free gaits of dressage, "no" hands are required for set periods of time. The horse is completely abandoned by the hand and must be able to retain his own pace and balance without support. This is not only difficult for long periods of time but also virtually impossible, and the gaits suffer, becoming strung out and either too hurried or too lax. Nor can a horse remain straight for long periods of time without guidance. Riding on a loose rein is an occasional relaxation for the horse, however, and it is also a good exercise for the rider's balance. Nevertheless, it is an exercise, and all exercises should be practiced only according to their schooling value. Loose-rein riding is not that valuable an exercise, and people who habitually ride cross-country on a completely loose, dangling rein are simply dangerous!

The ultimate hallmark of sophisicated riding is the educated hand, and it is years in the making. The educated hand is not only able to regulate pace and direction smoothly, like the good hand, but also has the infinite nuances and variations necessary to correct faulty carriage in the horse. In fact, the educated hand has such controlling powers over the forehand of the horse that, in practice, the head can be placed wherever the rider wishes it to be.

Needless to say, the educated hand is only developed through vast experience. Only familiarity with a variety of mouth problems and their relation to carriage and balance problems in general will teach the rider to use his hands as a correcting element. And of course, the educated hand also requires the support of a good seat, legs, and balance at all times. Head carriage cannot be influenced unless the horse's whole body is being influenced. The forehand must be corrected for the haunches to respond. The educated hand is a hand responding and counteracting, by minute punishments and rewards, to the horse's drive forward to the bit, a drive imposed by the horse's energetic temperament or by the rider's legs and seat.

### THE FIVE REIN AIDS

Hands are more versatile than legs; they have infinite shadings and degrees of control and therefore are the most sophisticated of all the aids. Their infinite nuances can only be learned through feel and experience on many horses having different mouths, and it is therefore sufficient to categorize the rein aids into a general group of five: the direct rein, the indirect rein, the leading or opening rein, the pulley rein, and the neck rein. (A variation of the direct rein that we'll discuss separately, because of its overwhelming—and to me, mystifying—appeal, is the vibrating hand.)

The basic hand-rein relationship, outlined earlier in the discussion of the position of hands and arms, is the direct rein, the means by which collection or a decrease of pace is customarily obtained. Its most important characteristic is straightness of the horse's head and neck, with no evidence of bending or flexing to either side. In its simplest form, this rein control retains a straight line from the rider's elbow to the horse's mouth at all times, regardless of the horse's head position, head placement problems being corrected by the rider's driving aids and not by an incorrect hand position. However, for certain specialized performances, such as the showing of a hunter, the hands may remain low even though the horse raises its head producing a broken line below the mouth, in this instance in order to convey an impression of the casual ease with which the horse may be ridden. Even more useful, for short periods of time, is the high hand, which creates a broken line above the mouth and is often effective in correcting and elevating horses with heavy forehands.

The indirect rein, the second rein aid of importance and supplementing the direct rein, controls lateral work such as bending or turning. In going from a direct to an indirect rein, the inside hand moves above and in front of the withers, or above and behind the withers, causing the horse's head and neck to bend toward the inside just enough for the corner of the horse's eye to be visible to the rider, no more. This same rein also displaces the horse's weight from the inside to the outside shoulder, thus affecting the balance from side to side rather than from forehand to haunch as is the case with a direct rein. As the inside rein, for example, the right rein, moves to the top of the withers, the left hand shifts correspondingly to the left, yielding to the same degree that the inside hand takes up. From a direct rein with five ounces of pressure in each hand, if one were to apply a right indirect rein, one would now have about seven ounces of pressure in the right hand and three ounces in the left. An indirect rein is used for all the lateral work, and care must be taken, when applying the indirect rein, never to cross over to the other side of the neck. If the rider feels this temptation, a common one, he should use more leg to supplement the rein aid. While an indirect rein in front of the withers displaces weight to the opposite shoulder, the indirect rein behind the withers displaces weight from one shoulder to the opposite haunch. Again, the way to judge correctness of position of this rein aid is by a line from the inside of the bit through the withers to the horse's opposite hip. As far as its general purpose is concerned, it is most used for any two-track lateral work such as haunches-in and two-tracking, or any work where the horse must bend in the same direction he's moving.

The third kind of major rein aid, the opening or leading rein, are categorized together, since they act upon the same principle. The leading rein opens farther to the side than the opening rein and does actually lead the horse around the turn. An opening rein merely opens out to the side, never back, and is used to guide the horse while the leading rein turns either a very green horse or very balky horse. Each of these aids should be thought of solely as directional reins having nothing whatsoever to do with bending or restraining. Flexible riders of a sensitive nature tend to utilize these rein aids a good deal as they direct and encourage the horse rather than force him.

In contrast, the fourth, or pulley, rein is an aid of tremendous severity which is used for emergency control at fast paces only. In its application (which requires a bit of practice before one attempts to use it during the galloping work for which it is intended) the knuckles of the inside hand are pressed down into the top of the withers and active control is left to the outside hand, which acts backward and upward. The more the outside hand pulls up, the more the inside hand pushes down, sometimes even sliding over to the other side of the withers, making an extremely sharp stop control. Be sure to fix the inside hand, not the outside one, as this alteration helps to keep the horse from becoming one-sided. Also, when riding in a ring, turning the horse's head toward the wall gains the advantage of an additional stopping block. Great care and judgment must be exercised in regard to the stopping, or pulley, rein, as it is very severe, and because of this characteristic association with a rough hand, it is not, as a rule, considered appropriate for refined riding at show gaits. Out hunting, however, where emergency stops are a necessary part of the game, it is definitely apropos, as it is in hunter hack classes where a hand gallop and stop are required. For sharp turns in the woods or during a handy hunter or a jumper class, a pulley rein is useful. In this case, for turning, one sets the outside hand and brings the horse around with the inside hand. Generally, however, it should be considered an extraordinary measure and reserved for such use.

The application of the neck rein, the fifth rein aid, is fairly simple. Both hands move over in the direction of the turn, which causes the outside rein to press against and even cross the horse's neck. It is not surprising that this rein aid is a commonly used western control, for it demands a prompt turn of the animal's shoulders by its bearing action, hence the name "bearing" rein. I do not teach or advocate this rein aid for normal hunter or equitation riding, but restrict it to sharp turns in jumper time classes where the emphasis lies on speed and instantaneous response, regardless of technique. No points are awarded in these classes for sophisticated subtlety—the fastest wins, and in this case the neck rein often comes in handy.

Two interesting variations, although not rein aids as such, are the vibrating hand and the lifting hand, both of which act as an accent strengthening the direct rein. In the vibrating effect, the hands rotate back and forth, with a slight sawing motion, thus counteracting stiffness, fixation, and heaviness in the horse's jaw. The lifting hand corrects horses that are either overflexed or "boring" down on the bit. This lifting action is best used in a series of jerks upward, the strength being determined by the degree of the horse's resistance. As soon as the horse ceases to offer any of these defenses and becomes soft, carrying himself and his rider in light balance, the hand ceases to vibrate or lift, returning to a steady position. Only after developing a relatively educated hand, capable of providing both instant punishment of resistance and instant reward for response, should a rider employ these strong but effective rein actions.

In essence, the five main rein controls provide a base for the functions of the hand. They may be incorporated together or combined in different ways for various special effects, but the above-mentioned group alone will suffice for all the exercises encompassed in this book.

WEIGHT AS AN AID

Considered as an aid, the primary characteristic of the rider's body weight is its intimate association with the hand and the leg. Weight cannot be used alone; it must be used in conjunction with the leg which drives, or the hand which restrains. Actually it is impossible for the hands or legs to be used altogether independently of weight, and however imperceptible the weight aid may be, it is always there.

The rider's body influence travels down through his seat bones into the horse's back. The seat, therefore, not only is a base of support, but also becomes a center of communication to the horse's "motor" which is his back and hind legs. This point of control, in relation to the "motor," is vital, and it becomes obvious why the hands and legs must be in partnership with weight to be effective. A common sight is the rider perched above his horse. His legs are weak and helpless as a driving force; his hands work to no avail as a retarding force. It is impossible to start, stop, or turn without some weight shift. Positioned in the lightest, most forward seat, weight manifests itself through fixing the knees and thighs.

Even to the untrained eye, the effect of weight becomes especially apparent when the rider's upper body is behind the motion of the horse. Swinging with the movement of the horse, the rider's weight becomes a driving aid; when he braces his back against the horse's movement, his weight acts as a holding or restraining aid. Thus weight is a primary control in all kinds of riding, for it can exert a decisive influence on all the other aids. Diligent attention through specific exercises must be paid to it from the start in order to develop independence and balance. Riding without stirrups is the surest way to obtain a strong seat and a feeling for weight distribution, as we've already discussed.

## SPURS

The spur (whose use is often abused, with or without knowledge) simply accents the leg aid. Those riders who willfully lack consideration for the spur's severity are no more than "butchers," while riders who cling on by heel and spur through ignorance or lack of balance are hardly better. The sole occupation of the spur is to support and follow up the leg's action. Especially if the horse is not very responsive to milder pressures, a nudge with a spur can teach him to respect the leg aid. Let me state here that spurs are not for the beginning rider or even many intermediate riders, especially over jumps. One should permit a spur only on a rider with an educated, independent leg, a leg that will not involuntarily "hit" the horse.

Correctly worn, the spur rests at the top of the heel, just under the heel seam of the boot. Often, one sees the spurs worn at odd angles, sticking up or drooping down rather than horizontally placed, usually with the intent of increasing or decreasing the force of the spur with a particular horse. This not only looks unattractive, but it is also a dead giveaway to any horse show judge, actually advertising the horse's problem of sluggish response to leg signals. The answer, of course, is a different spur— shorter, longer, duller, or sharper. Any aid that attracts attention to itself over a period of time should be replaced, since it becomes obvious that some problem still exists with the horse. This is true of the natural as well as the artificial aids. Overuse of any aid adds an element of crudity to any riding performance.

### THE STICK

The stick, whip, or crop is the most powerful of all the conventional aids, natural or artificial. (Needless to say, I do not propose to deal with such barbaric methods as the use of electricity, chains, and similar devices.) The stick itself provokes sufficient fear and respect through proper punishment to stimulate more than enough forward response. It arouses such response not only by some pain but also by noise, and this combined effect creates a powerful tool when dealing with any horse under most circumstances.

The correct use of the stick must be properly learned; like the spur, it is too often employed stupidly or brutally. Its simplest application consists of taking the reins in one hand, reaching back of the saddle and applying the stick once or twice and no more, and then returning the hand immediately to the reins. It is incorrect for the novice to hold the reins in both hands and hit the horse on the shoulder, since this will produce a definite clash of controls if the rider is not yet completely independent in his use of aids. (This shoulder method of using a stick can be very effective at an advanced stage of riding, when straightening and driving a horse forward at the same time. However, it is not for the novice.)

It is popular today to carry a rather short crop on a hunter, as it is less conspicuous, especially if it is a conservative dark brown or black. On jumpers a longer, regulation stick is naturally better, simply because it can do a slightly better job.

## USING THE VOICE

The voice, or "clucking" to the horse, is one of the most successful, widely used aids in driving the horse forward. Not only is it subtle and mild, but it complements stronger controls, encouraging instead of demanding. Clucking is really invaluable in conjunction with the leg, as it does not cause the tension or fear in a horse that a stick or spur might. Though it is a happy intermediary force between the leg and the artificial aids, the wise rider still uses this aid with discretion; its overuse quickly causes lack of response and reflects the rider's weakness or timidity with regard to other aids.

Clucking becomes effective and meaningful for the horse through association with the whip. A conditioned reflex is established by applying the stick and simultaneously clucking while holding the horse at a standstill. Once this conditioning has been repeated several times, the horse will react to the noise of a cluck in exactly the same way as he does to a stick. With a horse of placid or lethargic temperament, this exercise must be repeated fairly often, or the association will soon be forgotten. But remember, clucking does not replace the leg—it strengthens it.

Like clucking, "whoa" is more of a request than a demand. Voice aids really don't have strength in and of themselves to constitute an order, and if used in a commanding manner they defeat their own purpose, since they are not meant to induce fear. (The crude or frightened rider who yells "Whoa" to his horse is most likely to get an increase in pace rather than a decrease!) Therefore the word "whoa" must evoke a conditioned response from the horse. The execution of a decrease is the most accurate conditioning exercise for "Whoa." The word should be spoken clearly but firmly, yet not too loudly, and the decrease should be made simultaneously. The end will have been accomplished when the horse comes back solely from the voice aid itself. From time to time, of course, the conditioning exercise will have to be renewed.

At all times it should be remembered that verbal controls are supplementary to the primary natural aids, and do not replace them. Overuse of voice aids is a cardinal sin, indicating the ineffective, weak, or timid rider.

## SUMMARY

The accurate employment of the aids, singly or in combination, is related to and absolutely dependent upon a strong seat, correct basic position, and natural equestrian balance. Without this secure position, indepence and control of each part of the rider's body is impossible. If there is not complete bodily control, literally down to the finger tips, it will not be possible to direct the horse accurately, let alone to achieve any of the accomplishments of advanced equitation in which endless nuances of control are demanded. The competent horseman uses his body as an instrument of communication, immune to any surprises provided by his equine partner, but able to so regulate and dictate the most precise commands to his horse that the horse-rider relationship is truly interwoven into one unit.

The acquisition of such control takes hours of work; the habit of sitting correctly requires exercises, strenuous or even painful ones, and these exercises must be given attention throughout the rider's lifetime. A correct and beautiful classic seat results only from work. And only when this has been accomplished can the rider be permitted to forget the form of his body and concentrate on its functions in riding. A horseman may be considered classic only if he does the job at hand and does it gracefully; the underplay and invisibility of the aids are what count! Many are riders; many are craftsmen; few are artists on horseback. What a thrill it is to see a Piero or Raimondo d'Inzeo, a Bill Steinkraus, or a Kathy Kusner at work, work that is the culmination of years of attention to detail. The riding experiences that follow the establishment of a sound, basic, technical foundation will be experimental ones, consciously or unconsciously. This period, after a basic technique has been acquired, is a most exciting one for the horseman, for the whole scope of the sport at last becomes available to him. However, the necessary preliminary to this is the mastery of the kind of exercises on the flat that are discussed in the next chapter.

Although the next section deals with the training of horse and rider only on the flat, it is as applicable to the rider whose principal interest is jumping as it is to the rider who has no desire to jump. Surprising as it may seem, only a small fraction of the problems encountered in jumping cannot be largely corrected by work on the flat, and most serious jumping faults stem directly from faulty basic positions or the rider's lack of understanding in the use of the aids.

PART TWO

# Work on the Flat

# 3
# Working Principles
# in General

Now that the rider's basic position and use of aids have been described in general terms, the time has come to consider their practical application in riding the horse on the flat and to discuss the different formalized schooling exercises and the working area in which they are performed.

## THE SCHOOLING RING AND ITS PURPOSES

All normal work for both horse and rider should be accomplished within the framework of a schooling ring, either a real or an imaginary one. As a practical matter, a dressage-type ring, with its particular tracks and specific lettered reference points, is probably the most convenient form to employ. The various lettered locations encourage prompt and accurate controls during flat work, and if the rider accustoms himself to working accurately within a confined space, he will find that he has much more control when working in an imaginary area in a large field.

The working area should always be a rectangle or at least an oval having two long sides and two shorter sides, and in the case of the rectangle, four right-angled corners. In use, the long sides and long diagonal tracks are used for work on straight lines and extensions, while the shorter sides are used for collected work. The corners are both a good starting point for work and, as they require a horse to bend and collect himself, a deterrent to the horse who tends to gather speed on the straight line. The diagonal lines of the ring connect the opposite corners (actually starting about twenty feet from the corner), they cross the ring and terminate the same distance from the opposite corner. This way, there is time to make the horse take the corner in the correct fashion. Other lines of importance are the middle lines, bisecting the length and width of the ring in halves. Quartering lines in a ring are more for use in the dressage square.

Along with the basic tracks upon which the horse works, are the primary points. These points in a dressage ring are labeled A, X, C, etc. For hunter and jumper schooling such exact definition is unnecessary, although it is useful if the letters are posted. They encourage discipline and instill in riders the habit of specific execution, a trait too often lacking in most hunter riding. Naturally, most rings don't have letters posted and so it is necessary to establish points to memorize. These should be the middle points of both the long and short sides, and X is generally accepted to mark the exact center of the rectangle. The points of the diagonal lines should also be remembered. The rider who wishes to specialize in dressage should memorize the exact dimensions, lines, and letters of the dressage square. Dressage work is a great deal more regimented than other work, and in competition, the letters govern the entire ride. However, the point of this book is not directed at those who would go into dressage; there are already many good books dealing with dressage training.

Something of importance to remember is how to work in the wide open spaces. There are two ways to ride in large areas. One

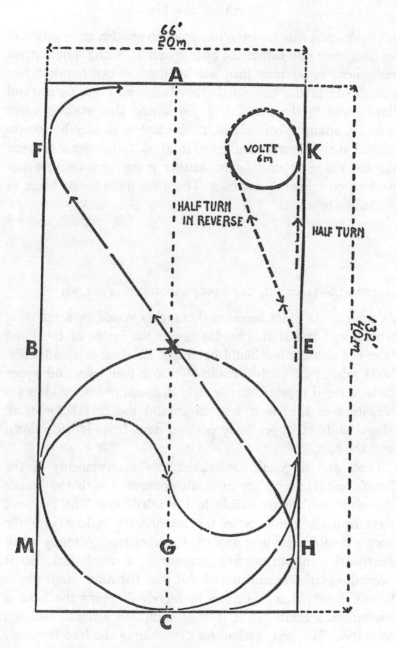

1. Lines and letters of a ring

is to ride cross-country from one point to another or to establish an imaginary ring within the open space. This ring should never really need to be more than one hundred by two hundred feet and should retain, through imagination, the same points and lines found in the actual ring. By having this working space mentally arranged beforehand, more exact work may be accomplished in an otherwise undefined location. Often riders are seen vaguely riding around fields, neither going cross-country nor working on schooling exercises. There are not enough hours in the saddle to waste!

DIAGONALS—LEANING, LOOKING, GLANCING, FEELING

As soon as the rider becomes thoroughly versed in actual ring terminology and is able to distinguish the inside of the horse from the outside, he should be taught his diagonals and leads. Most riders pick up bad habits by using their eyes and upper body to see if they are on the right diagonal or lead, and in anticipation of this, it is wise to control the eyes beforehand. Many faults of upper body posture stem from looking down with the eyes.

Leads and diagonals are related to the movements of the horse's legs. Here we are primarily concerned with the horse's shoulders, as they are visible to the rider's eye. The first and most common tendency in the beginner is to lean over the horse's shoulder and peer down at the front legs. Not only is this unattractive and an extreme measure for a simple task, but it jeopardizes balance and control and puts the rider ahead of the horse's motion. Looking down by merely dropping the head is less serious a fault, but it is amateurish and seriously detracts from style. The best method for determining the lead is merely to glance down. The rider does not drop his head, but only the eyes to the top part of the horse's shoulders, and so balance and

1. *Riding an equitation class.* Jim Kohn's eyes and head are up and looking straight ahead; his back is practically parallel to that of the horse while there's a perfect line from rider's elbow to horse's mouth. The leg, too, is ideal: contact is distributed equally between thigh, inner knee bone, and calf; the ball of the foot is resting on the middle of the stirrup allowing the heel to be driven down; the rider's toe has turned out ever so slightly in accordance with his own conformation. PHOTO BY BUDD

2. *Riding a hunter*. Even though Raymond Burr has lost his leg position a bit in the air, he still gets my vote as the most classic riding professional ever. Shown here on the great working hunter Kimberling, Raymond was equally at home on jumpers, proving to all who watched that good form and good riding can and should go together. PHOTO BY TARRANCE

3. *Riding a jumper*. The concentration, following hand, and beautifully held leg shown here are always present when Bill Steinkraus jumps fences. It was thrilling to me, personally, that a man so committed to good style should win the Olympic Gold Medal. PHOTO BY UDO SCHMIDT

4. *Olympic winner*. While very few win Gold Medals or are presented the King's Cup by Queen Elizabeth herself, Bill Steinkraus would agree, I'm sure, that his little day-to-day victories, such as getting a horse to flex at the poll or a first really good school over a complete course with a preliminary jumper, are almost as thrilling.

5. *What it's all about and how to get there.* If riding were all horse shows, bright lights, and blue ribbons, I'd have quit long ago. This picture clearly tells the true story of what riding means to me, be it competitive or for pleasure. Here a rider works hard all by herself in a remote corner of a field. She doesn't need an audience; her satisfaction will come from improving herself and her horse.

6. *Testing stirrup length from the ground.* A fairly accurate way of obtaining the correct stirrup length before mounting is for the rider to place his finger tips at the stirrup bar and measure the stirrup iron tautly from his armpit.

7. *Testing stirrup length when mounted.* Another testing method is for the rider to let his legs hang down to their full length whereupon the bottom of the stirrup iron should hit the ankle bone or just below it.

8. *Medium stirrup length.* This is about the length of stirrup I advocate in this book: short enough to allow plenty of ankle flexion yet long enough to keep the rider working out of her crotch in the front of the saddle, a nice combination of security for the rider and freedom for her horse.

9. *Short stirrup length.* This would perhaps be my limit for a short jumping leather; any shorter would suggest a racing leather, offering too little length of leg for real security or control. This particular photo offers good opportunity to study four principal angles of body control: hip, knee, ankle, and elbow. Notice how these angles close up as the stirrups become shorter.

10. *Long stirrup length.* While ideally I'd like this seat nearer the pommel of the saddle and the lower leg drawn back a bit, the whole impression is one of deep strength. It is, in essence, a seat designed for maximum control and contact between horse and rider. Notice how open her four major body angles are.

11. *Correct basic position at a standstill.* The rider sits so that a line from her shoulder falls directly down through her hip bone to the back of her heel. She is really in balance and in the middle of her horse, giving the appearance of being completely at ease and in control regardless of what difficult situation may arise.

12. *Good leg position.* A close-up of what we want: the ball of the foot is on the stirrup, the rider's heel is down and to the rear of the girth, and contact is maintained through the inner knee bone and calf. If the toe were forced out any more, calf grip would result, while toeing-in would tend to loosen the calf. Notice the stirrup iron, which should be perpendicular to the girth and the verticle stirrup leather.

13. *Foot placed forward and "home" in the stirrup.* Not only is it impossible for the rider's upper body to be smoothly "with" his horse when his leg is in front of the girth, but heel flexion is also greatly diminished when the rider puts his foot "home" in the stirrup.

14. *Calf out with pinched knee.* Acting as a pivot, the pinched knee prevents enough weight being dropped into the heels and makes steady calf contact with the horse's barrel impossible.

15. *Correct upper body position.* Looking straight ahead, the rider is erect yet relaxed. Her shoulders are neither pinched forward nor drawn too far back and there is a true line from her ear through shoulder to the hip bone.

16. *A round, dropped, roached back.* Not only is this particular fault sloppy and unattractive, but it also undermines the correct use of the back, making it difficult to stretch the spine so that the full action of the rider's weight can go down through the seat bones and influence the horse.

17. *Correct hands and arms.* It is this straightness of forearm and wrist, with the thumbs just inside the vertical and a couple of inches apart, that produces elastic control from rider's elbow to horse's mouth.

18. *Wrists cocked and elbows out.* A particularly obvious example of a common fault found to a lesser degree in many riders. By twisting the wrists and allowing the elbows out, the soft mouth-elbow line becomes awkward and stiff.

19. *Eyes down.* It is interesting to see how weight distribution and balance are affected by the rider's eyes, which, having dropped, pull the head forward and down and roach the back. Directional movement and automatic riding reactions will be greatly hampered by this serious fault.

20. *Two-point contact.* This term simply states the physical relationship between horse and rider, the two points being the rider's two legs against the horse's barrel. Notice how there is no weight at all through her seat in this galloping stance.

21. *Upper body at the walk.* Having moved off from a standstill where her body should be absolutely vertical, our rider has shifted forward several degrees. It's a slight shift and that's all it should be at this gait.

22. *Upper body at the slow sitting trot.* Here our demonstrator is sitting very tall, deep in the saddle, and with a firmly braced back, producing a picture of great strength ready to accelerate or retard without delay.

23. *Upper body at the posting trot with the motion.* It is clear that the rider is inclined forward more over her crotch and the front of her seat bones. In posting from this position she will be thrown forward and up by the horse's thrust and the rider need do very little work.

24. *Upper body at the canter.* Seated just in front of the vertical, the rider is deep in her crotch, with that heavy, glued quality similar to the position at the walk and sitting trot. Let me point out that the extra protrusion of buttock is due to this particular rider's conformation and not in any way an indication of a hollow back.

25. *Upper body at the hand gallop.* A two-point stance, with the rider's weight displaced from her seat into her heels, knees, and thighs, is a correct galloping position. During the posting trot, hand gallop, and jumping, the upper body should have approximately the same forward angulation.

26. *Upper body at the posting trot ahead of the motion.* This rider is so far ahead of her horse's center of gravity that she has really abandoned any use of her weight. Feeling the possibilities for evasion in any direction, the horse soon learns how best to take advantage.

27. *Upper body at the posting trot behind the motion.* In contrast to the previous picture, this rider is posting from her hips vertically. While this position produces great drive and strength, often needed for extended gaits, it is not nearly so smooth as when posting with the motion and has little use in polished hunter riding.

28. *Basic position without stir-rups*. Almost identical with the basic position at a standstill with stirrups, the only real difference is that with stirrups, which act as a slight brace, the rider can produce a bit more flexion in the ankle.

29. *How to cross the stirrups correctly*. Notice how the buckle has been pulled down about eighteen inches before being crossed over the withers and turned upside down. If this is done properly, there will be no annoying lump against the rid-er's thigh.

control are maintained and style left intact. The eyes do all the work, invisible to the onlooker. For the advanced rider, the diagonal or lead of the horse may be felt in the horse's body, but it is not advisable for the beginner to attempt to tell his diagonal or lead from feel alone.

To repeat, the rider should glance down for his diagonal or lead, and once he is accomplished in this method and wishes to experiment in telling without using visual means, he may feel. There is no urgency in accomplishing this, however, and glancing will suffice. Leaning forward over the horse's shoulder, dropping the head to look, or any other contortions should be avoided.

Some people are confused by posting to the trot on a certain diagonal, and curiously enough others are not. The time required to learn diagonals varies more than for any other phase in the process of teaching. Some riders pick it up in six minutes; some take six months. Leads seem to be easier. I do not intend to go into the motions of the horse and his balance to justify the diagonal or lead the rider takes. Here we are interested only in the mechanical process of posting correctly on the outside diagonal.

As we have suggested, the rider glances at the shoulders of the horse. In establishing the correct diagonal, the focus should be on the outside shoulder in relation to the inside. As the horse moves off into his regular trot, the rider responds to the backward-forward motion of the shoulders by rising out of the saddle in conjunction with the outside foreleg's step forward. In other words, as the rider is out of the saddle, the horse's outside foreleg is at its farthest in front of the horse. Change of direction calls for change of diagonal; the rider sits in the saddle for one beat or step and rises to the opposite diagonal. This is all done without disturbing the beat of the trot. Once this is seen and understood by the rider, it is automatic. Diagonals are necessary for a truly straight and balanced horse, but are often underestimated, even by knowledgeable horsemen. This is usually a result of ignorance or laziness with regard to the small technicalities that are part of the polished horseman. (One is said to be posting on the left diagonal when the rider is rising out of the saddle as the horse's left front leg is moving forward and up. This is true whether he is working on a circular or a straight track. The same is true in reverse when posting on the right diagonal.)

## LEADS

Leads are easier for most people to recognize than the diagonals. Once diagonals are learned the leads seem simple. The lead denotes the leg on which the horse is leading while cantering. The canter is a lateral gait, so one pair of legs is always ahead of the other (opposite) pair at this gait.

In exactly the same way as at the posting trot, the rider glances at the horse's shoulder, this time the inside shoulder. As this shoulder precedes the outside shoulder, he will see that he is on the correct lead. The only exception to this is, of course, the counter canter or false canter. In this case, the outside leg leads rather than the usual inside one.

As in learning diagonals, the rider must be constantly reminded about his eyes. The danger of leaning over and finding the lead becomes more of a habit than finding the diagonal at the trot, since the body is tempted to lean slightly forward in the canter anyway. This tendency must be discouraged.

## SPEEDS AT THE DIFFERENT GAITS

Before we become involved in exercising flat movements and preparing for jumping work, it is helpful to establish the different gaits and their speeds in miles per hour. Not only is it important to become acquainted with each gait and its characteristics for schooling, but it is also important to learn speed in relation to these gaits in order to judge pace. Elaborate explanations concerning the tracks of the horse at different gaits are unnecessary here, but what is important is the basic understanding and use of these movements.

The walk is a four-beat gait at which the horse travels about four miles per hour; the collected and extended walk respectively reduces the speed to about three miles per hour or increases it to five or six. The ordinary walk, for the most part, is our main concern, and this is a gait used for limbering before faster work, rest during work, and cooling out. The free walk is an abandonment of the regular walk and is executed on a long, loose rein: no contact is maintained.

The slow and collected trot, although both are conducted at about six miles per hour, are distinctly different in tempo. The slow trot is a trot lacking impulsion and is, therefore, a decrease not only in speed from the ordinary trot but also in liveliness. This form of trot work is used to encourage obedience and is useful in aiding young or inexperienced riders to sit the trot, with or without stirrups. It is not a formally recognized or helpful exercise at advanced levels of riding. The collected trot, on the other hand, is something quite different. This gait, which is slower in miles per hour, maintains its active tempo, the same rhythm found in the ordinary trot. In order to execute this properly, the horse must always be on the bit and well versed in the action of both hand and leg; it is work of a highly sophisticated form that often proves detrimental to hunter schooling. (Open jumpers, in contrast, benefit a great deal from almost any kind of collection or extension.) As the rider's expertise enlarges, he will almost automatically substitute a proper collected trot for a lethargic slow trot when need be. It isn't necessary to press the issue, as the slow trot is adequate for the levels I wish to cover here. To become obsessed with dressage more often than not confuses and discourages the hunter seat rider.

The ordinary trot, regardless of whether one posts or sits to it, is conducted at about eight miles per hour; an extended trot at about ten. The ordinary trot is the two-beat working trot and is rightly named, as more time is spent at this gait than at any other. Not only does the ordinary trot offer the horse more muscular exercise and development, but it is also the most useful in helping him unwind and relax. Most basic and preparatory training is done here and it is therefore considered the foundation gait.

Unfortunately, because of the comfortable control attached to trot work, the canter is often neglected, and this is bad, seeing that most jumping work relies on canter regularity. The ordinary canter varies between ten and twelve miles per hour; the extended canter attains about fourteen. The canter in its most natural form is a three-beat gait, and if a fourth beat is heard, it is from a lack of impulsion and must be corrected. The true collected canter, as with the collected trot, is rather too sophisticated and unnecessary for the average hunter, though for the jumper it can only be beneficial.

Both the hand gallop and the racing gallop have their purposes—the hand gallop for fast cross-country or simulated hunter performance and the racing gallop for what its name implies. The hand gallop travels anywhere from fourteen to sixteen miles per hour, and anything beyond eighteen is considered a racing gallop. Unless there are specific reasons, such as developing fitness or agility and obedience at faster speed, little work is needed for the hunter at the gallop. Slower work, as a rule, is more advantageous. However, for the open jumper, controlled schooling exercises at the gallop are most advantageous, in fact almost mandatory now that so much in competition is decided on time.

### PUNISHMENT AND REWARD

Most of the rider's concern with his own position and his physical controls have now been covered as far as flat riding is concerned. From now on, controlling the horse and schooling exercises will be the main object, and the rider will be considered only insofar as he is the directing influence.

The heart of all animal training is conditioning response through punishment and reward. Only through understanding the punishment-reward process is it possible to evoke consistently reliable performances from the horse. Because of the limited degree of a horse's intelligence, it is necessary to train through repetition—not through sensational extravagances but through patience and sure methods. This kind of training produces obedience and relaxation through unity between the horse and rider.

We can define punishment as the use of any active aid. It should in no way be associated with brutality or violence, and degree fits the situation. Aids are thus a form of punishment. For example, to drive a horse forward, a slight squeeze of the leg is one degree of incentive or punishment, clucking at the same time a second degree, a spur another, and so on. It is well to keep in mind the scale of punishment during training, for too much or too little can be equally harmful. Remember, the maximum level of punishment is almost never necessary.

Reward, in contrast, is simply the lack of punishment; doing nothing, relaxing the active aid. Correct understanding of reward is infinitely more important as a training mechanism and kinder to the horse than a pat or carrot. Without reward, the yielding that counteracts punishment, true relaxed obedience is impossible.

To give an instance of punishment and reward, we squeeze (punish) the horse into an eight-mile-per-hour trot; he reaches the pace and the leg relaxes (reward). By closing the hand (punish) to decrease the pace, the horse stops and we relax the hand (reward).

The only pitfall to the understanding of the reward-punishment theory is human emotion. When temper and will power come into play and override intelligence, patience and everything else go out the window. Thought as well as talent produces riders; and good riders work through habit. Developing the habit of considerate punishment and reward shows signs of only one thing—good riding!

## PUNISHMENTS FOR DISOBEDIENCE

Punishment and reward is a general theoretical principle; each evasion of the rider's will, however, has its corresponding punishment. So once an over-all understanding of training has been accepted, it is up to the rider to isolate disobediences, learn their reliable corrections, or, in the case of the unusual, invent new ones. Since reward is always the cessation of punishment, and therefore completely reliant upon a preceding punishment, the degree and effectiveness of the punishment is a measure of the rider's skill. The more advanced one becomes in the art of riding, the more comprehensive will be one's means of dealing with evasions. These evasions need not be great—perhaps the slightest displacement of head carriage needs correction. All in all, riding capacity comes down to control, and control is commensurate with specific punishment in relation to specific disobedience.

## THE HORSE'S MOUTH

One of the most common areas in which to punish a horse is his mouth in its two distinct parts, bars and corners. The bars are the spaces between the incisors or front teeth and the back teeth or molars. The corners are, as one might suppose, the juncture of upper and lower lips. The corners and bars are sensitive and usually respond immediately to the punishment of the bit by an elevation in head carriage. If the rider is using the bit on the corners of the mouth, he raises one or both hands with quick, short nips or jabs and the head will follow. The abruptness with which this is done corresponds with the severity of the punishment. Punishing the corners of the mouth by raising the hands is less severe than punishing the bars, which is done by moving the hands down and out, with quick jabs of one hand only against the bars. Both produce the same result, raising the head, but pulling against the bars of the mouth means the rider must be very secure in his balance, as the horse usually stops suddenly and raises his head quickly. Since the rider's balance is forward against the pull of the bars, he may also be thrown forward and meet the horse's poll—head on, so to speak!

As with all punishments, those of the mouth vary in degree according to resistance. Determining whether the horse deserves the lesser or greater severity is up to the rider.

## BOLTING

Apropos of mouth punishment, bolting is a good example of a disobedience. This vice is usually greatly feared by inexperienced riders. Not being able to stop at will terrifies most novices. Since at one time or another a runaway will occur in every rider's life, it is best to have the correct remedy at hand from the beginner's first lesson in order to preclude any serious accidents.

The first step in counteracting the pull of a bolting horse is to lean backward and raise the hands, giving the rider a brace against the horse. At no time should a rider give in and drop his hands and lean forward. The second and most successful step in stopping a bolter is to turn the horse with one rein into a fence or wall, or any other large and substantial natural barrier, be it the side of a hill or thick hedge. In the absence of such a barrier, the only method is to set one hand on the withers and pull with the other hand, in a pulley fashion. This, and/or constantly forcing the horse to circle, will stop a bolter. Under no circumstances should this vice be allowed to continue, as it is a most dangerous habit. I strongly recommend more severe bitting on a known bolter, such as a double twisted-wire snaffle.

BUCKING

Bucking, another major vice which should also be quickly discouraged, is also corrected through the mouth. As a matter of fact, most disobediences are initially corrected through mouth punishments and then succeeded by riding forward. A horse cannot buck with any success if his head is up, nor is he apt to deal as jarring a leap if he is moving forward. One must, therefore, get his head up by mouth punishment and then drive him on ahead. Again, as in most other disobediences, the rider should lean back, behind the motion of the horse, in order to brace

2. Correcting a bolt with a pulley rein

against any downward pull of the horse's head and to be in position to drive the horse forward in front of him.

The immediate consequence of bucking for the novice is a fall, and although this result isn't desired, an occasional parting of the ways is a useful experience just to learn how it is done. Falls from bucks are not often serious, but a rogue or habitual bucker can learn to avoid being ridden by this vice and it should be nipped in the bud. Once a rider learns to stick out a buck and apply the proper corrections, great confidence is attained.

REARING

Rearing is a far more evil and serious vice than bucking. It is doubly serious because it can not only unseat the rider but also unbalance the horse and cause him to fall on top of the fallen rider. Rearing is not to be taken lightly and only an experienced, aggressive rider can mete out the proper punishment. Usually this vice has its innocuous beginnings with a balky horse who will not move forward. Sometimes this is a result of clashing of aids. The horse does not move out in response to the leg and refuses, in consequence, to take hold of the bit. Rearing comes about when the animal not only refuses to move forward but also wants to evade his responsibility actively and turn the other way. He indicates this by rising up and wheeling around to face the other way, this being the ultimate in rejection of the driving aids.

Again, the mouth is the source of the primary correction. Horses almost always rear up and to one side, trying to turn around. The first punishment should be jabs on the bars of the mouth, on the side opposite the way he is trying to turn. The opposite hand should be completely passive, hugging the neck. As soon as the horse drops down in response to the jabs in the mouth, he must be firmly and aggressively driven straight

3. Correcting a buck

ahead. This sequence of punishments not only chastises the horse for going up, but also keeps the horse straight and makes him go forward. This is important as it is easy to see that this habit is complex and sophisticated. Co-ordination and agility along with courage and determination are valued riding traits learned through necessity while dealing with a rearer or wheeler. In essence, good horsemen must have dealt with all of these vices satisfactorily at one time or another. Only after having dealt with major evasions are the subtler ones felt and understood. Let me say here that riders of limited experience should not be subjected to problems of this proportion knowingly. They will be challenged enough by average circumstance.

SHYING

Hopefully, most riders will not encounter runaways, buckers, and rearers very often, but shying is a problem often encountered by everyone. Horses shy for many different reasons, but chronic sufferers of the vice should have their eyes checked, and it is my belief that these horses, along with many hunters and jumpers who lack heart over fences, have eye problems. Eye unsoundness, I believe, is underestimated by many buyers and veterinarians. On the other hand, many horses shy out of sheer high spirits and freshness; nothing at all is physically wrong with them and the problem should cease with work. A definite diagnosis should be made if this habit persists or worsens as it is not only annoying but becomes dangerous and risky when jumping is involved.

Regardless of cause, I firmly oppose allowing the horse to stop and examine whatever is making him shy. This only accentuates his mistrust of the object and exaggerates its importance. It is most important to keep the horse moving forward on a circle or to turn him around and continue moving forward, back and

4. Correcting a rear

5. Correcting a shy

forth past the frightening object. While in motion at the walk, trot, or canter, the rider has the opening rein to hold the horse in the direction from which he is shying. At the same time, an inside indirect rein bends the horse's head away from whatever is causing him the fright. The inside leg vigorously attempts to hold the horse straight. In short, if a horse shies away from something on his left, the rider applies the same aids as he would for a right shoulder-in. In shying, horses tend to either increase or decrease their pace as they leave their track. Shying has not been eliminated thoroughly until the horse can pass the object without looking at it and with no change of pace. Although shying is a vice, the average case is rather minor, and most riders of elementary skill can be taught these basic steps as a corrective measure. If the problem persists to a disabling degree, the horse needs either more work or, as I've suggested, an eye examination.

SUMMARY

In essence, disobediences and their corresponding punishment close out this introductory chapter to flatwork training. By now the rider's terminology and understanding of a simple step-by-step technique should be complete enough to incorporate into his riding so that he can execute a progressive and worthwhile plan for an hour's ride. If nothing more, with little consideration as yet for the horse's education, the rider can think about and develop his own abilities. Very few riders take enough time to consider their own faculties and how they might be improved. But now is the time, with a solid foundation in proper training for the rider, to consider how to teach the horse a thing or two, and in teaching his horse, the rider of course advances his own education.

# 4

# Horse and Rider
# at Work — Longitudinally

All schooling movements can be placed into one or the other of two categories, longitudinal or lateral, and the distinction is a very important one to understand.

All the training of a horse that involves transition of pace or any collected-extended exercises on a straight line are considered longitudinal schooling movements. The horse is being suppled and made aware of the rider's demands; in this case, from front to back and back to front. He has made a lengthwise obligation to respond, and whatever demand be set forth in either of these directions must be considered longitudinal. Specific examples of longitudinal work would be a full stop, the extended trot, from trot to canter, or the piaffe (the trot in place).

Of equal importance, though totally different, is lateral training. Any exercise involving turning, bending, or moving sideways from the rider's leg or hand is considered a lateral schooling movement. The directional response, either right or left, categorizes this work, examples being bending through corners, a circle, shoulder-in, or a flying change.

Both of these schooling categories, lateral and longitudinal, must be worked in equal amounts and in logical sequence in order to insure the horse's rounded development and suppleness. There is nothing more frustrating to me than to ride a horse with basic gaps in his education. A good case in point would be the horse who makes a beautiful simple or flying change yet still falls on his inside shoulder around a corner. Don't just school your horse in the movements you enjoy best; work on his collections and extensions along with bending right and left. Now let us consider longitudinal work in more detail.

PACE CONTROL

Regardless of the kind of riding, the level of riding, or the horse being used, the first necessity is control over pace. Being able to slow down, speed up, stop, and start not only fall under the category of basic control, but also have the most subtle influence on performance, so that they are prime determinants of victory and defeat even up to the very pinnacle of equestrian sports. Nothing, not even head carriage, suppleness, or response, is sufficient excuse for a weakness in pace control. Every means must be employed to obtain this control, and thus the more elementary the rider's ability, the cruder and more artificial his supplementary aids are. Of course, the ultimate test of a rider's skill is his simplicity, and the test of a flat rider's ability is the dressage test, done in a plain snaffle bridle, completely void of artificial bits or martingales. However, riding at this level is for the dressage artist. Other forms of equestrian sport, because of their speed and split-second physical controls, do not allow time for these relatively deliberate aids.

Once pace control has been established and remains a permanent factor, the paths are laid open to addition, subtraction, multiplication, and division—the higher mathematics of riding—but always control the pace!

### INCREASE OF PACE

Pace control, as we have said, is so paramount in all phases of riding, is so much a part of the beginner's safety, and so determining of every level of performance, whether it is the hunting field, the show ring, or the race course, that it must be examined as a subject to itself. My interest, aside from the control, is to make a smooth transition. Smoothness and invisibility are characteristic of polish and form, and the habits from which they stem must be established from the start; once they become automatic and are coupled with firmness, control in a pure form will result. Any violations of this principle, such as kicking or pumping with the upper body, not only are beginners' bad habits, but might also remain through all levels unless corrected.

Before the horse may be expected to move forward, he must have freedom of the head and neck. This freedom is conceded by what is termed the "release," relaxing and giving slightly with the hands. Once the horse has been released, he is able and generally willing to move forward in response to the rider's two legs. The action of the legs must be imperceptible, and a way must be found to make it so if it is not. A nudge with the spur is permissible but any form of kick is not, and those are the boundaries for leg control. Kicking is not only a rough, crude aid but also results in a loss of security when the rider abandons his calf contact in order to kick. In short, to augment an increase in pace, the rider squeezes his two legs together after having released his horse. If he doesn't receive a suitable prompt response, a slap with the hand or stick behind the saddle will evoke action. This sequence must be unhurried and yet definite, producing the desired result for the exercise to be satisfactory.

DECREASE OF PACE

The same standards must be met in slowing down or stopping. Abusive or exaggerated hand action appears to be more common even than the primitive attitudes of leg control and often a good deal more harmful to the horse. Good, bad, "no," or educated hands have been discussed previously, and while educated hands are possessed by few, good hands are within reach of every horseman. They are the property of all who are willing and patient.

Sympathetic, definite hand control again results from smoothness and persistent determination. In decreasing pace, the hand closes in much the same way as in squeezing an orange. The arm should not pull nor the wrist twist; only the hands and fingers close. Always in conjunction with the activated hand, the rider sinks down into the saddle in order to coordinate his weight as an aid. The rider waits for the horse to decrease or stop and, at all costs, resists the temptation to pull. Pulling and kicking are in the same category, rough and primitive.

The important thing in all equestrian matters is for the rider to wait for his horse. The rider must allow himself the discipline of letting things happen and not be in a hurry. If the horse is reluctant to slow down or to stop from the prescribed method, the hands must be kept fixed and closed and the shoulders permitted to stretch back of the vertical. Actually, if force should be resorted to, it is the strength of the rider's back and weight that ultimately controls the horse, and this holds true for the increase as well as the decrease of pace. Weight should not, however, be evident in normal, controlled conditions. It is more apparent under duress, and when great demands are being made on a horse's balance and agility.

**HALT**

Of all schooling movements, the halt is probably the most often performed, yet regardless of the degree of horse-rider proficiency, this exercise is rarely executed well cnough. It could always be done better, and this even seems to be the case at the highest dressage level. The basic, fundamental difficulty inherent to the halt is the lack of motion. When the horse is stationary, the rider has difficulty in overcoming any evasions by means of forward motion. Of course, the range of exactness connected with this movement is enormous. Relative to the rider's skill and horse's training, whether it is a beginner simply trying to stop any old way, an intermediate attempting an even, straight, prompt halt, or a high school dressage rider's perfect, square, full stop on the bit, disobediences, ever so slight, crop up. Basically these show themselves in four ways: not stopping and standing still, not remaining straight, not being square and evenly balanced on all four legs, and not taking the bit. As each level of accomplishment is reached, more and more of these characteristics should be eliminated.

Almost simultaneously with achieving the indicated pace control at the trot and a primitive bend around the corners of the ring, the rider starts teaching his horse to halt. The rider closes his fingers around the reins, thus fixing his hand and stopping further forward movement. As the horse decreases his pace to a slow trot and a walk, the rider sinks down into the saddle and opens up his body. This is what is commonly known as bracing the back, and how important it is! For within this braced action lies the strength and control of the rider's weight over the horse's weight. The braced back evolves from the rider's slightly stretching and arching his shoulders back, while keeping the small of his back fixed forward and his seat bones glued into the saddle. Another way of describing the use of the back is to tell someone to "stretch his spine and vault his chest." Pulling the horse back, jerking, twisting the wrists, or sitting abruptly down in the saddle are wrong. The transition should be smooth and invisible, and the horse will soon respond to the closed hand and braced back, the basic co-ordinators responsible for the full stop. As soon as the halt is completed, the rider relaxes his hand and his back as a reward for obedience. This relaxation should in no way resemble a sloppy loss of form and position. It should be a merest softening of the more tense braced back.

Naturally, as we have said, there are many problems in this movement. The possibilities of minute evasions are numerous, and some of the more common ones will be discussed here along with the remedies.

Actually, getting the horse to come to a stop is often a challenge to a beginner. The solution never lies in pulling, but rather in the correct use of the rider's back, and in persistence by making certain the hands are closed and fixed. The horse always will stop through strength of the rider's weight, and often this necessitates leaning back behind the vertical. If these two forces are constant and uncompromising in their effort, the most stubborn borer will come to a standstill. The point is never to lean forward and give with the hands until the horse has stopped.

A reasonably straight, square halt must be demanded even at an elementary level. And by insisting on a straight stance, the rider automatically becomes introduced to the four corners framing the horse's body. These four corners provide four avenues of escape: right shoulder, left shoulder, right quarter and left quarter, aside from the horse simply backing up. As soon as the horse drops a shoulder off the track, the opposite rein must counteract this. As soon as a quarter goes off the track, the corresponding leg puts it back in place. The framework of control is the four-cornered relationship between the rider's legs and hands. Absolute squareness and true perfection of head carriage are properties of dressage, and are, I believe, too sophisticated technically for hunter seat work. As long as promptness, smoothness, immobility, and straightness are obtained, enough has been accomplished. It is hard enough.

BACKING

Backing rhythm resembles walking in reverse and should be like the ordinary walk in straightness, promptness, animated cadence, stable head carriage, and, later on, backing with a specific number of steps in mind. The back follows the full stop, and it's very important not to allow the horse to move one step backward until he has stood still for a few seconds. Then begin backing. As soon as he has backed the predetermined number of steps, he should resume forward movement without any interruption whatsoever. In other words, it is wrong to allow the horse to stop after he has backed a certain number of steps. It breeds evasive habits, especially getting behind the bit as well as behind the leg. The walk back and resumption of the successive gait should flow all together as one movement. In short, a proper back up is a continuous motion as follows: the horse halts for about three to four seconds; he backs a specific number of steps (three or four); he immediately resumes the desired gait or moves forward into line and repeats the halt.

The initial function of the aids is to prohibit forward movement, therefore requiring the same closed hand as for decrease of pace. The horse is at a standstill, the hand closes as if squeezing an orange while the legs become active, causing the horse to move into the bit. The horse, unable to move forward because of the fixed hand, yet wanting to escape the leg pressure and bit, is forced into walking backward. As the horse backs, the rider's shoulders open up, staying on the vertical so that the weight of the upper body acts as a driving aid. The cardinal sin is to allow the body to fall or lean forward, permitting the horse to escape behind the rider's driving aids, his legs and seat. A fundamental riding principle is for the horse to be ahead or with the rider's center of gravity, never behind it. Until the horse has completed the desired number of steps, the hand remains closed and the legs actively squeezing. Once the steps are fulfilled, the hand rewards the horse by yielding, releasing the horse to go forward from the pressure of the legs. During the entirety of this exercise, the rider's eyes remain forward and up so as to feel evasions of straightness and regularity. If the horse does not remain straight and displaces a haunch to the side, the corresponding leg is used.

Backing is not only an exercise useful within itself as a means of reverse, but it also is helpful to lightness and collection, acting as a gathering force. Its stress and emphasis are toward the haunches, and because of its rather taxing strain on the hocks, care should be taken to keep the steps smooth, regular, and unhurried. I do not believe in backing as a means of punishment except in cases of severe rushers, but all horses and riders should be acquainted with this exercise at a rather early stage.

### CANTER DEPART

Of all aspects of riding, the canter depart is certainly one of the most controversial. This is undoubtedly due to each writer's own level of experience, the kind of riding he is committed to, and his experience in other exercises. Actually, I am sure everyone wants the same result—a prompt, clean, straight depart. Now, most horses are conditioned to ready obedience and, with any natural balance at all, willingly strike clearly into the canter from the given aids. The dispute, therefore, revolves around straightness and how best to obtain it. Unfortunately, horses in

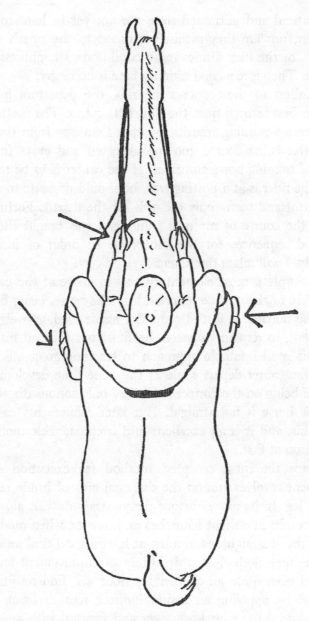

6. The canter depart

their natural and untrained state are not yet in harmony with the rider, nor are they precisely attuned to the rider's signals, balance, or the like. Under these conditions, straightness is impossible. Therefore a good training base is necessary.

Regardless of the sequence of aids, the departure into the canter is best learned from the slow sitting trot. The posting trot encourages a running transition rather than one from the walk. The latter is, of course, too sophisticated and exact for early stages of training horse and rider. If the canter is to be required while the rider is at a posting trot, he should decrease to a slow, sitting trot and then apply the aids for the depart. Fortunately, during the course of my own training, I was taught three distinct aid sequences for the canter-on. In order of increasing difficulty, I will relate them here.

The simplest, most elementary way to arrive at the canter is by the use of the outside rein and leg. The horse, being bent toward the outside, is forced onto the inside lead by weight displacement; to remain balanced, he must put forward his inside leg. This is an infallible approach to teaching green riders and horses the canter depart while at the same time developing the habit of being on the correct lead. The only serious drawback is that the horse is not straight. But later refinements can overcome this, and it is an excellent and irreproachable method of instruction at first.

Perhaps the most accepted method for execution of this movement revolves around the diagonal aids of inside rein and outside leg. In its more obvious demonstrations, this aid combination results in a slight haunches-in; however, when modified, a fair degree of straightness results, at least a good deal more than with the first method. It is definitely an improvement for showing, and even quite an elementary rider will find results easily obtained by applying an inside indirect rein in front of the withers and driving his horse over and forward with an outside leg.

The third, most sophisticated canter depart results from an-

30. *Corrective exercise position without stirrups.* While this young lady's upper body is carried to perfection, she has allowed her knees to come up so that her seat is pushed too far towards the rear of the saddle.

31. *Hand on hip exercise*. After the rider has abandoned the security of holding the pommel, this exercise seems to be the easiest in attempting complete independence. Plant the hand firmly on the hip with the thumb behind the back. Again, don't let the knees and thighs come up as much as this.

32. *Hand behind back exercise*. Practicing this exercise can encourage good posture by the rider's pressing the middle of the back with the free arm. Take care not to jut the chin forward and down as this girl is doing.

33. *Rotation of arm exercise*. From this position the rider may attempt several valuable suppling movements. Two of my favorites are: rotating the arm in big slow circles, keeping the upper body stationary; and keeping the arm fixed as the trunk rotates from front to rear.

34. *Touching the toe exercise*. This is one of the greatest limbering exercises. In the beginning it is permissible to draw the leg up towards the rider's hand. But the point is to stretch the upper body as much as possible while keeping the leg fixed.

35. *Horse fitted with longeing attire.* The reins of the simple snaffle bridle are knotted in the mane so as not to slip and the side reins are comfortably adjusted just below the reins. Notice how the longe line is attached and be sure to use the proper whip.

36. *Rider being longed at the trot.* This is a good exercise for teaching the rider to follow the movement with the small of her back, demanding complete independence of leg, hand, and seat. Her toe is out too far, causing calf grip and raised knee, but her shoulders are in a good position, being parallel to those of her horse.

37. *Cantering on the longe in a forward seat.* To cross over and touch one's toes is one of the most taxing of exercises on the rider's thighs. Not only does this work strengthen the galloping position, but it is also a great confidence builder.

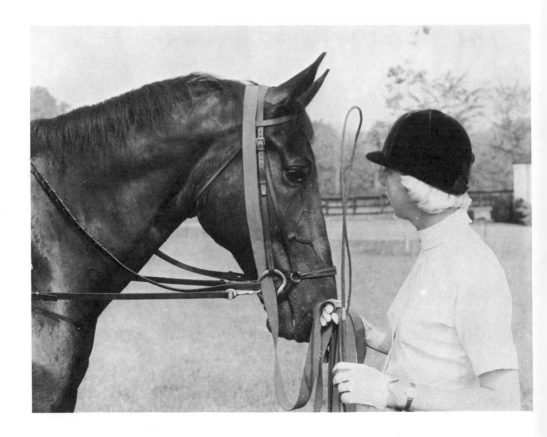

38. *Looking ahead at a specific focal point.* Our demonstrator is using a tree as a focal point for stopping on a straight line. While looking directly at the tree she can still see everything around her with peripheral vision.

39. *The rider using her eyes on a turn.* The horse is turning to the left, bent to the left, and the rider is anticipating this turn by looking ahead to the left. This mare, however, is above the bit and lacks flexion, and this fault has developed what is known as a muscular "under-neck."

40. A *driving or bending leg.* This rider's toe is turned out considerably in order to get maximum use of her spur. In this position, just at the back edge of the girth, the leg acts either to drive or to bend the horse.

41. A *displacing leg.* The rider's leg is displaced to the rear for the purpose of a turn on the forehand. Notice the right indirect rein supporting this leg aid.

42. *Using the leg in horse's shoulder.* While this is a rather uncommon leg aid, it works wonders in counteracting a horse's tendency to fall against the inside shoulder. Since it may cause a loss of balance in the rider, I'd save it for advanced work only.

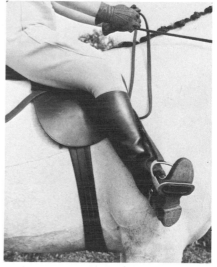

43. A *direct rein*. This is the most basic of the five rein aids, acting from the horse's mouth straight to the rider's elbow in order to decrease pace or to back. Remember that the hand is always activated by closing and holding, not by pulling.

44. An *indirect rein in front of the withers*. Displacing weight from one shoulder to the other, this rein aid bends the horse in the head and neck only. An indication of its correct positioning is a line from the inner side of the bit through the withers to the rider's opposite hip.

45. An *indirect rein behind the withers*. The girl's right inside hand is correct for this rein aid, though I'd prefer her outside hand to be lower. Generally I find the hands work best when carried at about the same height. Note the difference in line, from the horse's mouth to the horse's opposite haunch, rather than to the rider's opposite hip as in the preceding rein aid.

46. A *leading or opening rein*. The action of the hand to the side and not to the rear is clearly apparent.

47. A *pulley rein*. This rein aid acts as a lever. The knuckles of the inside hand fix upon the withers while the outside hand works upward and to the rear.

48. A *bearing or neck rein*. This rein aid acts as a wall against the outside shoulder, so that the horse has no chance of escaping a turn by bulging to the outside. Notice the rein pressing against the horse's neck.

49. *Cantering behind the motion.* This is a good example of a situation in which the rider has fallen slightly behind the vertical, which enables her either to drive forward or to hold back.

50. *One way of wearing a spur incorrectly—pointing up!*

51. *Another way of wearing a spur incorrectly—pointing down!*

52. *Using the stick on horse's flank.* With the reins bridged into the opposite hand, the rider applies her stick back of the saddle to reinforce her leg.

53. *Leaning over.* The wrong way to check one's lead or diagonal.

54. *Looking down.* Dropping one's head is also unnecessary.

55. *Glancing.* Not only is this a sure check of a lead or a diagonal, but it is also subtle and invisible.

56. *Mouth punishment in the corners*. The rider raises her hands with slight jabs to punish the horse in the corners of his mouth.

57. *Mouth punishment on the bars.* By lowering the hands and using slight jabs, the rider affects the horse's bars.

58. *A halt.* The mare is straight, square, and immobile, and also alert.

59. *Backing up.* This shows resistances—tail swishing, ears back, mouth open, stiffness of poll and jaw.

60. *Using the pulley rein in the gallop and stop.* While the inside hand becomes fixed just in front of the withers, the outside hand works upward and to the rear.

other set of diagonal commands. Both the rider's legs are in contact and the reins serve solely for collection; bending is non-existent. The steps of application are as follows: the rider supports his horse with his outside rein and positions his outside leg back; he collects his horse and, at the desired moment for the depart, activates his inside leg just at the back edge of the girth; his inside rein remains passive, its only job being to keep the head from bending out. The horse is mostly controlled by an inside leg and an outside rein, and, as in all riding, he is being pushed by this leg toward the outside hand. This evokes the most nearly straight transition, and, as long as all four actions of both hands and both legs are understood, difficulties are unlikely to occur. Once the canter is easily achieved from the slow sitting trot, the rider should encourage the horse to canter directly from the walk and the halt, keeping the horse as straight as possible from head to tail. No bending of head and neck nor displacement of haunches should be visible.

While there is so much dispute and feeling centered around the canter depart, in reality any aid combinations will do that provide a transition suitable to a particular purpose or level. Straightness, promptness, and lightness exemplify prowess in equitation and dressage, even though their perfections need not be seen in the hunting field.

FROM THE CANTER TO A SLOWER GAIT

In the transition, bringing the horse from the canter to the posting trot, the slow trot, or the walk, the rider strives with his aids to make the break as smooth as possible. I have singled out this downward transition, since it is rarely done well. After attaining the slower gait, rhythm and the cadenced trot or walk should be established as promptly as possible; and in the case of advanced demonstration, immediately.

For example, the horse is cantering along and the rider wishes to decrease to a posting trot. The rider collects his horse, bringing him back to the regulated ordinary trot. Often it is seen that the horse breaks into a hurried, lurching trot before coming to the cadenced gait, or, just as commonly, he props forward onto his forehand at the moment of transition, jogs a few steps, and then must be urged faster. Both of these actions are symptoms of lack of co-ordination between driving aids and restraining aids, and usually a slackness and sloppiness of the rider. There are three precise steps to this particular transition: the rider collects his horse's canter by closing his hands, bracing his back, and holding with his legs. He then asks for the break into the ordinary trot by another half-halt with his hands. Once the horse actually changes to the new gait, the rider must be on guard with hands and legs to insure that proper rhythm, pace, and impulsion are maintained.

## GALLOP AND STOP

Of all exercises necessary for the well-schooled hunter or jumper, this is as important as any. Being an abrupt transition of longitudinal discipline, it will not particularly appeal to the more refined dressage rider. Those, however, who hunt, ride cross-country, or are involved with any jumping work whatsoever know how invaluable this quick response is. With practice, the gallop and stop can become refined and smooth within its own limits, which are not quite those of the classic *haute-école* standard.

Aside from its practice out hunting or on the open jumper's training grounds, this movement is an often required test of the hunter hack or equitation rider. The demand for precision and obedience put to the test, both the horse's manners and the rider's control and stabilized headwork is required of both. The rider, having put his horse into the canter, moves out to a controlled hand gallop, assuming his two-point galloping seat. Several strides before the appointed halting point he sets a pulley rein and, depending upon the horse's degree of response, applies the rein aid. The less responsive the horse, the earlier the rein must be applied, assuring a stop at the exact point. In addition to this rein aid, the rider may, in a hack class only, say "Whoa" in a clear voice. Voice aids, in general, detract from the rider's invisible controls, and they should be kept to a minimum during equitation classes. An occasional cluck and an inaudible "Whoa" are permissible as long as they don't replace the more corporal aids.

After the horse has become fully acquainted with this stop, a direct rein may replace the pulley rein. The well-schooled hunter hack should stop on a dime with just a low quiet "Whoa" and very little rein aid. Dropping the reins and walking the horse back to line on the buckle are both very effective displays of manners in this type of class. Equitation riders, on the other hand, ought to retain their form, tidiness, and control at all times.

## STRONG TROT

The strong trot, a preparatory exercise for the more advanced extended trot, is useful in that it evokes a forward response and a lengthening of stride, both of which are definite attributes to the hunter or jumper. The stronger, faster gaits tend to loosen and relax, providing they are practiced in accordance with each horse's specific disposition; some settle down through extended exercises and some heat up. Knowledge and experience can tell the difference.

In execution, the rider may either post or sit this trot, insuring maximum drive. In a rectangular dressage ring, because of the relatively narrow dimensions, it is best to sit through the corners and short sides and drive the strong trot down the long sides, posting a bit behind the motion. This is not necessary, however, in a regular oval ring; the balance and cadence of the strong gaits are easily maintained around the gradual turns, and continuity would be lost if collection were injected at this time. During a U. S. Equestrian Team equitation class, for example, the strong posting trot would be held the circumference of the ring. No interruption or change of pace is necessary until the next gait is called for. Swing and thrust, along with an increase in pace, are characteristic of this gait and should be looked for. Allowing for the rider's slight upper body erection, there should be no position change, and smoothness and invisibility of aids stay intact. Strong gaits are excellent riding exercises in that they encourage the use of both the rider's back and his legs to propel the horse forward.

Once the horse is on the bit at the ordinary trot the strong gait is easily obtained. By slightly relaxing the feel on the horse's mouth and activating both legs, the horse will lengthen his stride and increase his pace. However, care must be taken by the rider so that the strong trot stays cadenced and no unevenness or hitching creeps in. If this should happen, the hands must steady and balance the trot a bit while the legs maintain the forward drive.

## STRONG CANTER

Of similar nature is the strong canter. It is preparation for the extended canter and its characteristics are thrust, pace increase, and lengthening of stride. This particular work has especially good results in settling a high-feeling horse who likes to play but is basically of docile disposition. Allowing this very particular type of horse to move out and get rid of the kinks does wonders!

The strong canter's execution has a sequence similar to the strong trot's. The rider collects and balances his horse through square corners and short ring sides, and along the long sides he drives out the extension. Again this transition is unnecessary when riding a large oval ring. A mistake often made by riders is the assumption of the forward seat. A proper strong or extended gait, under classic terms, is ridden with a deep, full seat and not in a light half-seat. It is best, whenever cantering in any form in the show ring, to remain seated and to assume two-point contact only during galloping work. For this reason, all canter work and gallop work must be separated, so weight displacement and seat position may be correct.

The opportunity to become acquainted with a horse's temperament is probably best afforded by the strong gaits. When a horse is asked to increase his pace, his personality becomes quite obvious. A horse of average temperament will require no more than a relaxation of the hands and a closing of the legs for a strong canter. A sluggish horse, on the other hand, requires a release plus leg and weight drive, or spurs, a cluck, and perhaps even the stick if he is a real dullard. The tense, nervous animal is just the opposite. By riding him more through driving aids, matters grow worse. All this animal needs is an easing off of his mouth. Just release. Through experimentation at pace transition, riders learn to feel just how much or little is needed to evoke a change in pace.

SIMPLE CHANGE

Of all cantering exercises, perhaps the most elusive in its perfection and deceptive in its apparent ease is the simple change. This is one of those schooling movements that everyone knows they should do and teach every horse even for the most ordinary hacking purposes, yet even at the better riding levels the simple

7. A simple change of lead

change displays severe riding faults. The neglect surely results from the fact that all riders effect a simple change of some kind, and therefore never retrace their steps often enough to perfect this elementary and basic demonstration of control.

The simple change, a longitudinal exercise, may be examined during the diagonal cross of the ring. The change occurs at the middle point of this line and should be straight, smooth, and prompt. The horse cantering around the ring on the right-hand turns diagonally toward the center of the ring after having gone through the corner. Several strides before the middle of the ring he is brought back to a slow trot or a walk, depending on the horse's degree of collection. After crossing the middle point of the ring, he is put onto the other lead, the duration of the transition being three or four strides. The important point for the rider to feel is the change of his own legs. As the horse approaches the change, from right lead to left, the rider's outside left leg holding him must change and become the inside driving one; simultaneously his right leg goes back a hand and becomes the supporting holding leg. The outside reins change in order to support the horse. Straightness must be the result of co-operation between both legs and both reins, keeping the horse framed. Promptness is a follow-up to obedient response and a clear understanding by the horse of the rider's intent. The finished performance must be smooth and the aids invisible.

During the early stages of training of either horse or rider, it is best to encourage changes during turning patterns. Figures best suited for the incorporation of this movement are the figure eight, serpentine, half-turn, half-turn in reverse, and the change through the circle. The directional movement followed by the horse helps advise him as to the correct lead. Of course, sooner or later all horses should be so versed in the aids that any number of changes may be practiced in succession on straight lines. By this time, the change of the rider's legs is enough to indicate to the horse the correct departure, the hands serving only to maintain a straight forehand.

# 5

# Horse and Rider
# at Work — Laterally

## BENDING IN THE CORNERS

Once the rider is aware of his first training obligation, pace control, and has established this control, horse and rider are ready to follow a prescribed track around the edge of the ring. Our major concern here is riding the corners and bending the horse according to the turn throughout the length of his body. The primary lateral demand is to bend through the corners, and to encourage the horse to understand this exercise it is necessary to apply two rein aids and an inside leg. Let me point out here that while initiating a very green or young horse in this exercise, great care must be taken to round out the corners in a gradual fashion, and under no circumstances should an attempt be made to square them acutely. When approaching the corner (and the slower the gait, the easier it is to learn the co-ordination of aids), the rider applies an opening outside rein. The effect of this rein aid inhibits the horse from cutting the corner, keeping him on the desired track. A directional aid, the outside rein in no way bends the horse, however. The rider next applies an inside indirect rein that does bend the horse in the direction of the movement. Almost simultaneously these rein aids are combined with an inside leg, bending the length of the horse's body and pushing him into the corner. The rider should not be glancing at his hands, but rather looking around the corner himself, feeling the application of aids. As far as the outside leg is concerned, it remains on the horse behind the girth, functioning as a supporting guard. Should the haunches swing out away from the track, thus diminishing the bending action of the inside leg, this outside force is used. Any other similar evasions off the track must be counteracted in the same manner, by the use of diagonal aids. Also, in their attempt to escape the hand or leg longitudinally, horses tend to increase their pace or, occasionally, decrease their pace. Pace control, as mentioned, is most important to maintain here.

A correctly bent horse must also track accurately. By this I mean each hind footfall must follow its corresponding front footfall and the horse's weight must be evenly distributed among all four legs. This measure of control and proper riding prevails through all regular schooling movements done on one track, that is, left hind following left front and right hind following right front. Of course those exercises done on two tracks such as leg yielding, shoulder-in, haunches-in, and the two-track itself are something else again.

CIRCLING

The circle, a lateral exercise, follows the bend through the corner. A good way of introducing the green horse or young rider to the circle is by making it a continuation within the corner. Since riding through a right-angle turn makes half the circle, continuing the bend results in a complete circle. From the point of view of lateral flexion, the corner contributes much in preparation to the circle. This, however, is merely an introductory means to circling and is not essential; circles are and should be made any time and place.

Being really the most basic of all the lateral schooling figures, the circle presents the foundation for all other turning exercises. It solidifies all eye work and is most successful in instilling discipline, both from the point of view of aid co-ordination and in teaching horse and rider exactness and duplication of ring figures.

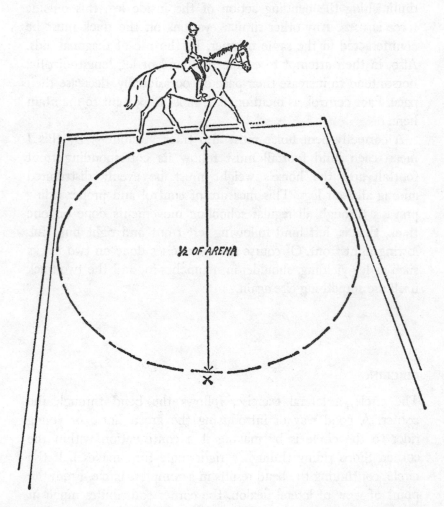

½ OF ARENA

**8. A circle**

In making a circle: The rider prepares for the turn by a slight steadying of pace; his eyes being constantly ahead of the track of the circle, the inside leg and rein keep the horse bent to the inside while the outside rein holds the horse's pace and the outside leg guards against the horse going outside the track. The smaller the circle, the more the horse is bent throughout his body. There are two ways the horse evades the track of the circle, by cutting in or bulging out. When the horse cuts into the circle, the rider applies an outside opening rein and an active inside leg. If the horse bulges outside of the track, the rider's inside opening rein becomes active and he holds the horse with the outside leg and supporting rein. Let me repeat the form of a horse correctly bent from head to tail: The horse's head is bent to the inside just enough for the corner of the inside eye to be visible; his neck bends correspondingly in order to follow the head; by the action of the rider's inside leg pushing into the horse just behind the girth, the horse's body bends around this leg; and last but not least the outside leg, about a hand behind the girth, holds the haunches in, thus creating a horse shaped like a half-moon or bow. During all of this lateral sideways concentration, care must be taken to hold the horse's pace even.

In short, circling is not only the primary lateral figure. It is also a great collecting, balancing exercise, and its value in schooling horses that hurry and rush is almost unlimited. Like the full stop, circling is something that should be learned early and repeated often.

FIGURE EIGHT

Simply joining two identical circles at a given point creates the lateral schooling exercise known as a "figure eight." This movement sophisticates the simple circle by having continual changes of direction, thus bending the horse alternately from his right to his left. Used for his bilateral bending work and in the exacting discipline of following two circular tracks of identical diameter, the figure eight becomes commonly one of the most popular lateral exercises.

As we have said, the eight consists of two round circles of the same size and executed at a given pace in a given area. The two

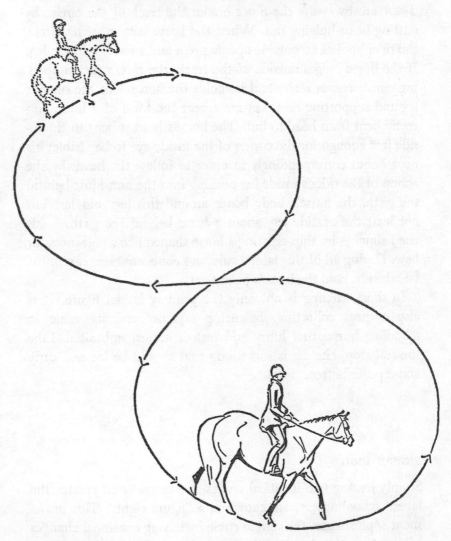

9. A figure eight

important points in riding this figure are the focal point and the point of intersection. The focal point is necessary for the rider to line up his point of intersection. It is beyond the intersectional point, where the two circles join, and is chosen by the rider from the available terrain. Again, as in any lateral exercise, we are interested in the proper bending around each circle and in accurately following the track of the figure. Use of the rider's eyes in this exercise is most important.

The dangers encountered in this movement are much the same as those in a circle; the horse may hurry or lag. While the horse remains bent in following the circles, he must be absolutely straight for two or three steps before being asked to bend in the opposite direction. The horse must begin and end the eight all at the same point, the point of intersection.

VOLTE

A dressage figure, rather foreign to hunter schooling, is the volte, a French word meaning "little circle." The volte has a specific diameter of six meters, or about twenty feet and is only interesting to us at certain times. The extreme handiness of a jumper, or perhaps an equitation horse, is benefited by the volte. It is usually performed at the collected paces, the slow trot and canter; its diameter being so small, it requires the maximum bending abilities of the horse. All the rider's aids similarly need to be at hand—a deep seat, an alert, active inside leg, along with a secure support by the outside rein and leg. Performed correctly, with balance, bending, and pace maintained, the volte in its perfect form is difficult indeed. Of course, action and promptness rather than minute perfection are the aims of jumper exercises, so practice the figure with this in mind.

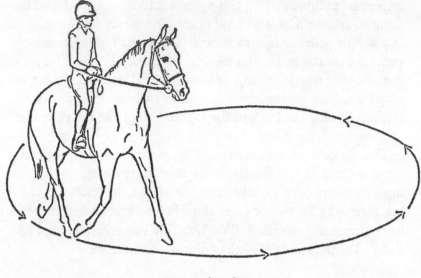

10. A volte

The attitude taken by the rider in performing the volte is exactly the same as in making a circle. The aids are identical, the only difference being the heightened awareness of collection and space, for the volte gives a feeling of constriction to the uninitiated.

## SERPENTINE

Another exercise of general interest useful in all training, as well as a frequent test in the show ring, is the serpentine. This figure is a series of loops bisected by an imaginary center line, the ends of which serve as both starting and finishing points for the exercise. Alternate bendings to the left and the right, separated by only a few straight strides between loops, present a challenge to the rider. The loops must be of exactly the same size and divide the ring, or pre-established boundaries, evenly. The eyes must be used to insure identical size loops, and pace control and proper bending of the horse along the track of the serpentine are necessary, all of which must be felt and maintained. Any changes of diagonal or lead are executed on the middle line; otherwise, the sitting trot or the counter canter is held throughout. The number of loops also must be definitely specified before the ride.

A typical test, often asked in the equitation ring, is to ride a serpentine of four loops the length of the ring at a posting trot and return at the canter, displaying simple changes of leads between the loops. The specific boundaries of the loops must be clearly understood beforehand. The starting point of this exercise would be the middle of the short side of one end of the ring; however, the rider's preparation would be a collected, sit-

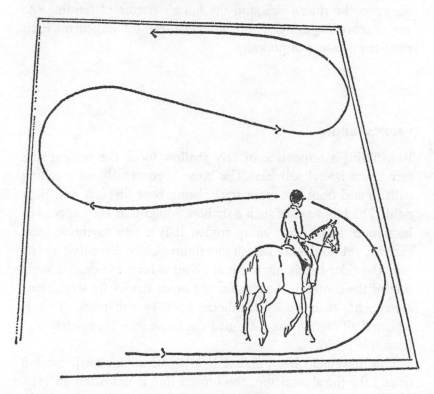

11. A serpentine

ting trot a comfortable distance before reaching the starting point, not establishing his ordinary posting trot and correct diagonal until actually hitting this point. Once the serpentine is under way, the rider concentrates on his tracking procedures, rhythm, bending, and prompt transitions and all the while maintains a symmetrical pattern until the termination point at the middle of the opposite short side of the ring where he makes a halt. This halt is only necessary in that it acts as a framework, ending the figure in a neat, controlled fashion. Once the canter has been started, the next series of loops are performed in similar fashion, except that now the major concentration shifts toward making a smooth simple change of lead between loops, a change either through the slow, sitting trot or the walk, depending upon the rider's skill and the horse's degree of training. As both a schooling exercise and an official test, the serpentine is an excellent measure of progress.

BROKEN LINE

Resembling a serpentine of very shallow form, the broken line serves as a lateral softener. The horse is constantly on a rolling path to and from the main track, being bent first left and then right. The loops are of such a shallow design that they appear to be zigzags, lacking any sharp angles. It is a very rhythmic, easy exercise, yet results are felt almost immediately. Executed at any gait, the rider bends his horse at about a forty-five-degree angle toward the center of the ring for five or six strides; he straightens a moment, then bends the horse back to the track. This is repeated all around the ring until the horse feels completely soft from side to side.

This movement has a unique training advantage for horse and rider. Like the shoulder-in, the broken line is not often an exercise judged in competition, but rather a training gymnastic.

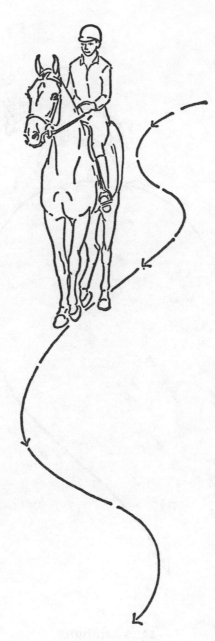

12. A broken line

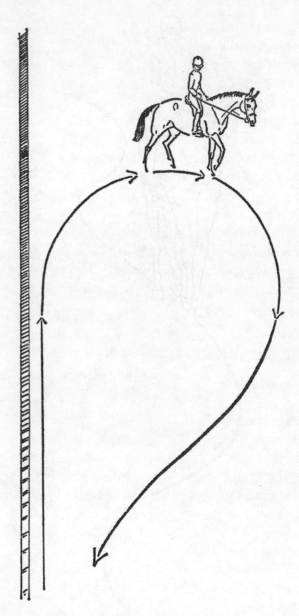

13. A half-turn

Thus, a variety of combinations of aids achieves the same result. Of course, the primary object of teaching the exercise is to cultivate suppleness and response to the inside rein and leg, causing the horse to bend in the direction of movement. This is the standard approach but by no means the only one. Other useful and interesting responses would be achieved from an inside leading rein and an outside leg, perhaps to steer a very young, green horse; or an outside bearing rein combined with an outside leg, especially employed for the horse that bulges. Even the alternating pulley rein effects an excellent exercise demanding quick manipulation, and in actual practice is resorted to by riders in the hunting field when going through thick cover at fast paces. With a bit of imagination and experimentation an otherwise rather secondary exercise can be quite useful, and even higher levels of training can utilize it at the counter canter or with flying changes of lead.

HALF-TURN AND HALF-TURN IN REVERSE

Both of these schooling patterns are vital to any hunter or jumper schooling; not only are they useful lateral exercises on the flat, but their actual tracks are often followed jumping a course. Both the half-turn and half-turn in reverse offer opportunities for the introduction of some new and more difficult exercises into a schooling program such as the counter canter, the flying change, and the two-track, all of which are easily taught within these turn patterns.

The difference between the half-turn and the half-turn in reverse almost always offers confusion to the novice rider. When drawn and seen ridden, both patterns are easily remembered. The half-turn is a half-circle away from the side of the ring, returning to the side on a diagonal line and continuing around the track in the opposite direction. The rider changes his diagonal or

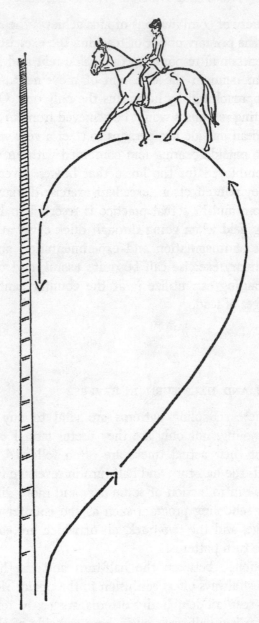

14. A half-turn in reverse

lead upon returning to the track. As we have mentioned previously, as in all lateral work, the importance is that the horse's body bends and straightens in accordance to the pattern being followed. There should be no crookedness on the straight lines or evasions in the turns.

The half-turn in reverse is exactly what it says. The rider goes away from the wall on a diagonal line, effecting his change of direction by turning back into the wall or track; he changes his diagonal or lead just before the turn back in. Again, the exception would be the counter canter. Both of these exercises allow great freedom of imagination and variety. Not only should they be done at the ordinary gaits, but the turns also provide opportunity for collection and the straight lines allow for extension of gait. Having the turn and the straight following one another so closely, longitudinal suppleness is required as well as lateral agility.

TURN ON THE FOREHAND

Before going any further, the horse must become acquainted with the displacing action of the rider's legs. He already understands the legs in terms of moving forward and bending laterally, as well as the holding action of the outside leg, but he has not really been taught to move his haunches sideways away from an active outside leg. The turn on the forehand is the most elementary exercise used to introduce this response.

By definition, this exercise means that the horse's haunches move in a circular track around the forehand, which remains close to stationary and acts almost as a pivot. This movement may be accomplished by diagonal or lateral aids, depending on the horse's advancement or the particular purpose for using this exercise. The bending either coincides with or contradicts the directional movement. Taking the easiest approach first, we'll demonstrate using lateral aids, outside rein and leg.

The horse is ridden parallel to the wall of the ring, a jump, or any solid barrier. His head is then turned, bent by an outside indirect rein toward the wall, and the rider's outside leg is displaced back. Holding the forehand still, the haunches are then displaced, step by step, around the fixed forehand. Of course, the number of steps depends on the horse's training. A step or two in the beginning is sufficient, although the average turn on the forehand is one hundred and eighty degrees. There are two common evasions in the exercise, moving sideways and moving backward. If the shoulder moves toward the inside, the rider's leg on that side becomes active at the girth along with the inside rein which acts as a bearing rein; when the horse backs up, the vigorous use of both legs and a straightening of the upper body takes place. The cardinal sin of all lateral exercise work is to have the horse evade the rider's will by dropping behind.

As soon as the horse understands and responds to this exercise, diagonal aids may be used. Of course, this means that the horse is bent toward the direction he is moving, and to do this he must clearly understand the different actions of both the rider's legs. An inside indirect rein predominates, supported by an inside leg to maintain bending while the outside rein holds the forehand still. At the same time, the horse must be moving away from the active outside leg in the direction to which he is bent. It is easy to see how such matters grow more complex. Not only must the horse respond by moving his haunches one direction, but he must also, in essence, contradict the direction with his forehand and respond with this part of his body in opposition. Realistically speaking, this more advanced method of turning on the forehand is only necessary for horses of higher dressage ambitions such as preparation for sophisticated lateral work, i.e., haunches-in, two-track, and so forth. For the average

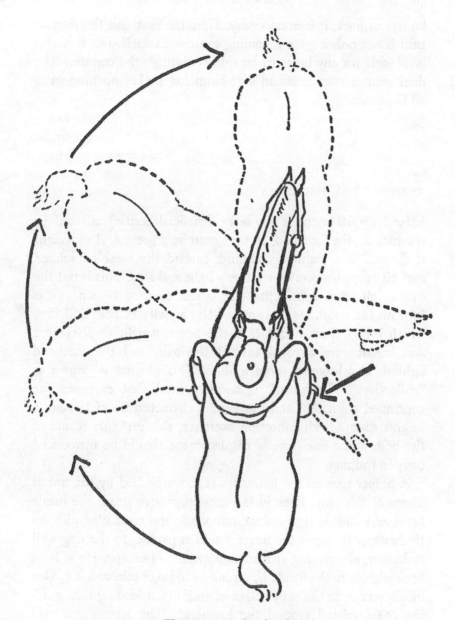

15. Turning on the forehand

hunter or hack, it is unnecessary. Here the first and the simpler turn is not only a good schooling exercise in itself, but it is also invaluable for any horse to be ridden through the country. The dual control over forehand and haunches makes opening gates all the easier.

### TURN ON THE HAUNCHES

Lateral displacement is the only beneficial control effected by the turn on the forehand. In that exercise a great deal of weight is directed in a stationary manner toward the horse's forehand and his haunches remain relatively light and free. This is not the case at all when considering the lateral exercise known as the turn on the haunches. Because of the activity of the hind legs, which brings them underneath the horse, weight displacement and balance are directed toward the rear, and the forehand lightens and becomes more mobile. This is what is known as "collection." "Gathering" is another word that expresses the continued animation and movement characteristic of the horse in this state. Of all collection exercises, this certainly is one of the best, and a few steps of displacement should be introduced early in training.

A proper turn on the haunches is accomplished by the use of diagonal aids only. Even in the most primitive stages the inside hand and outside leg predominate while the remaining aids actively support. Again the horse is ridden parallel to the ring wall or barrier, eliminating at least one avenue of escape. He is then bent slightly to the inside by an inside indirect rein and leg. This inside rein is, in the early stages of training, a leading rein, guiding the forehand around the haunches. The later stages will allow an indirect rein behind the withers, which is enough of a guide to directional movement for the initiated horse. Re-

61. *Strong trot*. Flowing freely forward, the horse is being balanced and driven by the rider's slightly more erect upper body.

62. *Strong canter*. Although this horse isn't as firmly on the bit as I'd like, it's obvious that he's gathered, balanced, and ready to stride forward.

63. *Bending through a corner.* An excellent example of a rider looking through her turn while her horse is bent properly from head to tail.

64. *Posting with the motion over an imaginary jump.* To learn the basic jumping controls, the beginner trots between two standards.

65. *Primary release (grabbing the mane) over a rail on the ground.* The security of having a little mane at this riding level insures complete freedom for the horse and confidence for the rider.

66. *Reins in the outside hand, mane in the inside hand.* My favorite corrective exercise position to develop leg and upper body control.

67. *Guiding (opening) rein in the outside hand, mane in the inside hand.* Also a corrective exercise position which allows the rider to practice separate activities with each hand.

68. *Eye control head on.* Using the instructor as a focal point is exactly how a rider should practice eye control.

69. *Eye control to the side.* Concentrating on the instructor at the side of the jump is an excellent exercise to prepare for turns.

70. *A good picture of heels and legs.* Depth of heel and calf contact behind the girth characterize a good leg.

71. *"Ducking."* Any excess motion of the upper body can and should be eliminated. Teaching the rider to approach fences with the motion and with his eyes up will help to correct this unattractive habit.

72. *Leg too far back causing a "perch."* As soon as the leg slips too far to the rear, security and control of the upper body are certain to be lost.

73. *Two-point approach.* A galloping or half-seat should be used for most hunter and equitation work. The rider's legs rather than her weight support the horse's forward stride.

74. *Three-point approach.* Two or three strides from the fence this girl is sitting lightly in her saddle, supporting her horse's forward stride with both her legs and upper body weight. While riding with weight insures more control, freedom and smoothness can suffer.

75. *Secondary release—resting on the crest.* In the intermediate release the rider rests her hands a third of the way up the horse's crest and actually presses down, providing the support still needed at this stage of riding.

76. *Using the stick at a standstill.* Rather than just showing a horse a strange jump, condition him to go forward.

77. *Using the stick at take-off.* In dealing with major jumping hesitations, I've found that using the stick in this way gets the best results.

78. *A good jumping turn.* This horse's lightness of forehand and controlled outside shoulder and haunch guarantee a balanced tight turn to a fence.

79. *Good upper body in the air.* Minimum of motion and an approximate parallel of the rider's trunk and the horse's top line usually indicate good upper body control.

80. *Jumping on an angle.* The rider's eye control and the ability to keep a horse on the bit are absolutely necessary in preventing run-outs while angling jumps.

81. *Not enough release.* This is what is known as a "set" hand and is certainly not liberal enough in its release of the horse's head and neck.

82. *Eyes down*. Both the balance and feel are undermined when one looks down while in the air.

83. *Dropping back too early*. When a rider's seat is actually in the saddle before the horse lands, she's definitely interfering with the horse's back action.

84. *A poor jumping turn.* This rider is really asking her horse to go to his forehand by dropping her eyes, shoulders, and hands.

85. *Jumping "out of hand."* Keeping a feel of a horse's mouth for turning in the air is a good way to introduce jumping "out of hand."

86. *Correctly knotting the reins in the mane.* The safest way to eliminate reins for work with no hands.

87. *Hands to the side over a multiple in-and-out.* The rider's reins and stirrups have been taken away in order to achieve an absolutely independent leg and seat.

88. *Hands on head exercise.* Notice the beautiful leg position.

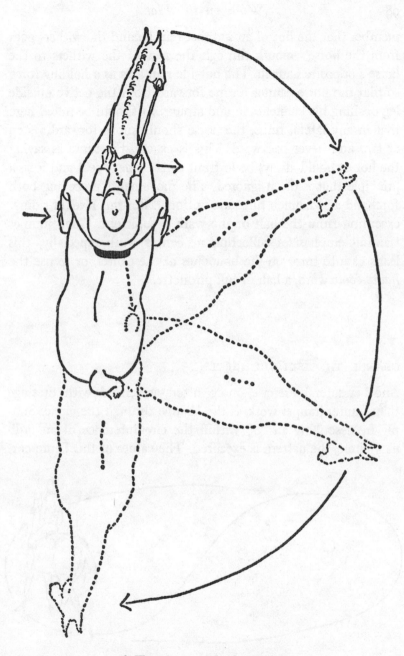

16. Turning on the haunches

member that the line of an indirect rein behind the withers goes from the horse's mouth through the rear of the withers to the horse's opposite haunch. The outside rein acts as a holding force so that the horse cannot escape forward from the active outside leg pushing his haunches in and around. It should be noted here that in any lateral turns, the horse should move forward a step or two and never backward. This is exactly the same as saying the horse should always be in front of the rider's seat and legs, a principle that is often ignored. The movements preceding both forehand and haunch turns are optional. For this level of riding, execution from the halt or the walk is sufficient. Good jumper training emphasizes collection at canter work especially; this leads us into turns on the haunches at the canter, or to use the *haute-école* word, a half or full pirouette.

CHANGE THROUGH THE CIRCLE

Another lateral exercise, more often associated with dressage than hunter-jumper work, is the change through the circle. Simply by describing an "S" within the circumference of an ordinary circle, the pattern is executed. The values of this figure cor-

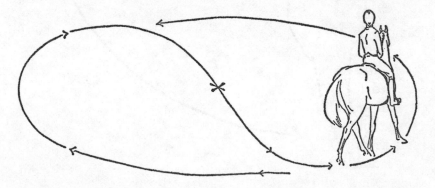

17. Changing through the circle

respond to those of serpentines and figure eights, namely, the alternate bending combined with several straight strides. A simple means of reversing direction and providing a nice practice track for simple or flying changes are added uses to this easy pattern.

## FLYING CHANGE

In most hunter-jumper work, schooling exercises are primarily a means to a well-rounded end and very few of these movements are directly influential during actual performance at faster paces and over fences. Their value, although important, is usually somewhat indirect. The principal exception to this is an important one—the flying change of lead.

The flying change of lead is the change of legs at the canter or gallop in the air. There is no interruption of stride nor any obvious change of pace, though collection and balance must be in evidence if a thorough change is to occur. It is easy to understand, in the light of pace continuity, how the flying change and actual conditions of performance go hand in hand. Really no other exercise is so closely integrated nor is any other exercise so ignored during the preparation of hunters and jumpers. Fortunately, the average horse eventually follows his instincts and learns to change leads around corners himself. Often this is not done fast enough for modern-day course design, and therefore special attention should be paid to this exercise before it can be expected to be automatic. A refined and quick flying change pays off in both hunting field and show ring, and in a perfect change both the front and hind legs of the horse change leads simultaneously.

As a case in point, we will examine the execution of the flying change on a half-turn on the left lead. As soon as bending is completed around the turn, the rider straightens the horse with his outside (right) leg and rein, almost to the point of bending him slightly to the right, an action that displaces his weight to his left side, thus freeing the right side. Having lightened the side toward which he wants to make the change, the rider holds the horse's pace, without allowing him to go faster or slower, and drives him to change with his new outside leg. This leg action occurs in the position of a displacing leg, about a hand back of the girth. The two most important characteristics of the flying change are straightness and pace maintenance. This is often difficult since horses learning this movement tend to try to run away from the rider's leg rather than shift laterally to the other lead. That is why I categorize this exercise as being lateral, not longitudinal.

18. A flying change of lead

Because of the frequency of flying changes during galloping work, practice should occur at this gait as soon as consistency shows itself at the canter. The aids are exactly the same: Make sure the horse is absolutely straight and his pace constant and activate the outside leg until the horse changes front and behind without any increase in speed. This should all be done in the rider's galloping seat, slightly out of the saddle; response here is from hands and legs, not weight. The horse, in essence, changes underneath the rider; when in a full seat, the horse moves in front of the rider. There is a difference in feeling and in purpose.

Once the rider and horse come into harmony with this kind of lead change, nothing appears simpler. As in the simple change, straight-line executions are only advisable after regular repetition of changes during turns. Again, during straight-line work, the aids are exactly the same, and it is up to the rider to feel how and where the horse is evading a straight track. Crookedness is a condition in itself, and often the corrections necessary interfere with the aids for the figure in question. Therefore the aids for a change of lead must be reinforced by those used to maintain straightness. In other words, both legs, both hands, and weight are always in use. None is ever absent.

COUNTER CANTER

In contrast to the flying change, the counter canter has no direct value to the hunter or jumper's performance; no one wants to jump fences off the wrong lead and that is precisely what this exercise is, practicing what is known as the "false gallop." Now, because this exercise, like many others advocated in this book, has no actual association with the specific equine sports of hunting and jumping, it does not mean that these movements haven't enormous value indirectly. From the point of balance and pace control, prerequisites to the counter canter, as well as the rider's strength of seat and independence of hands and legs, this exercise is excellent practice. Also, the horse's recognition of aids and obedience are tested rather severely while cantering different figures and retaining the false lead, and this is why it is a movement asked for in the U. S. Equestrian Team equitation class.

I find it easier to teach this movement following the half-turn. There are four distinct levels of advancement with regard to the counter canter: on a straight line; around one corner; along the short side of the ring or two corners; and a full circle. To initiate this movement, the horse should canter a half-turn on the correct lead, but at the point of returning to the track, where an ordinary lead change usually occurs, the horse is held on the same lead down the straight line, making a change only before the corner. If the horse does this easily, which he generally does, a gradual turn through one of the corners may be attempted. This turn should be very sloped and rounded; any sharp, square directional change at this stage will surely endanger balance, and a lead change is likely to occur. False cantering around both corners and the entire short side is generally no

19. A counter canter

more difficult than one corner, providing everything has been smooth and unhurried so far. By making the entire end of the ring an oval, elliptical line, the horse surely will not break to a trot or change leads. If he does, the rider must collect him to a slow trot or walk, wait until the next straight line that is the long side of the ring, and start again. Chances are it is too early to ask for a false canter depart on a turn; later on, yes! Once the horse and rider are confidently controlling the counter canter both ways around the whole ring, figures such as circles, figure eights, turns, and serpentines may be tried. Just as in introducing the new false canter balance through corners, it is most important to enlarge these figures a bit, approaching them through even, gradual stages. The greatest obstacle in conducting the counter canter is pace; pace or speed cause lack of balance which immediately intimidates the horse. His reaction to regain sure footing is to get back wholly or partially to his natural, secure lead. Through collection and control this won't happen, and soon the horse will feel comfortable and at ease, knowing he won't lose his legs around a turn. Of all exercises, this one must be approached in stages and with patience. Falls can occur.

As far as the rider is concerned while doing these exercises, he must be acutely aware of all his aids, their positioning and function. A deep, full seat is vital to balance the horse toward his haunches and off his forehand. The outside rein, which is now the rein toward the inside of the turn opposite the lead the horse is on, is used for full support. In the beginning stages, this rein supports with such definition as to bend the horse toward the outside. At advanced levels this is wrong. The horse, to be technically correct, bends toward the lead he is on while making any turn whatsoever, whether cantering in regular form or counter cantering. With equal support, and with predominant action over its inside fellow, the outside leg holds and maintains straightness throughout. The inside rein in the beginning acts as a guide and later on serves to bend the horse toward his inside lead, while the inside leg, positioned at the back edge of the girth, uses its influence as a driving force and, again at more advanced levels, to instill bending. As one can see, all four corners of the frame must be there, along with a constant weight distribution toward the rear. Any laxness on the rider's part will be paid for immediately; lateral figures of this difficulty do not happen in spite of the rider.

## WORKING ROUTINE

Every purposeful endeavor requires some system; the horse business is no exception. From proper stable management to the detailed schooling of a string of horses, discipline is a must. Without regulated work programs, mediocrity results, and in this scientific day and age there is little room for the mediocre. Even one who rides for pleasure should establish a concrete hourly plan that will insure technical progress and thus a greater degree of safety. And if this progress is to be ascertained and habits are to be formed, repetition becomes the most important element. Repetition of known and proved correct techniques brings results and there are no short cuts. Five minutes of a given exercise per day is much more beneficial than long-drawn-out attempts without schedule. Feeling and anticipation of a horse's moves and moods come from active practice and equine association much more often than, as the saying goes, from being a "born horseman." Talent, a combination of positive mental and physical qualifications, is all very well, but it in no way replaces work capacity or the desire to learn. The rider who works 90 per cent of the time and relies on natural talent 10 per cent will usually beat the one who skips along under the percentages in reverse. In sum, intelligent riding plans, divided most advantageously into hourly programs, expose the best within horse and rider, and in the shortest amount of time.

A preliminary routine of horse and rider at work could be

outlined as follows: After the rider has mounted (with his eyes up!), he walks off. While warming up at the walk, he assumes either a two-point contact and concentrates on holding his leg position, driving his heels down, back and in; or stays in his three-point contact, feeling the weight in his seat bones. When in the two-point contact, holding the mane or the martingale with one hand is a help. The rider controlling a good leg will be able eventually to walk in two-point contact position with both arms outstretched, his leg correctly positioned under his body. When correctly positioned in three-point, there should be approximately a straight line from the back of the head, through the shoulder, point of hip, and on down to the heel—HEAD, SHOULDER, HIP, HEEL. Used as a rule of thumb, this line assures good balance, just as the line from the rider's elbow to the horse's mouth predicts an elastic hand.

Now that the horse and rider have walked a few minutes, they are ready to go into the posting trot with the motion of the horse. This is the gait most desired, as it is at a controlled speed and yet still loosens both horse and rider. Aside from constantly positioning the rider's body correctly, the immediate goal is to keep the pace at a steady eight miles per hour—a lively trot, neither too hurried nor too slow. Let me repeat that this is only the beginning portion of an hourly working platform, perhaps the first seven or eight minutes. Additional practice in other associated exercises should take place almost at once, lest boredom and staleness occur. No one is so doomed as the rider who lacks imagination and variety in his work. Making a horse and rider, like building a concrete structure, is placing block upon block; each step requires a previous one.

In sum, horses get better or worse according to who is riding them. They do not maintain levels on their own, and vacillation, indecision, and ignorance create mediocre or poor riding and bad horses. The rider who goes for an hour's work knowing how to improve his form, aware of the correct aid application, co-ordination, and sequence for various results, and who has a variety of schooling exercises at his finger tips—this rider will do things well. He will enjoy hacking through the country, he will fox hunt with the best, compete favorably in the show ring, be able to school and develop his own winners. From every point of view, a comprehensive understanding of the sport has its rewards, whether safety, performance, or both.

PART THREE

# Work over Fences

# The Three Levels of Jumping

Generally speaking, it is pointless for the teacher to introduce his pupil to jumping even small fences until the sitting trot and canter are being executed well and a fairly high degree of independence has been established between the rider's hands and seat. Once this stage has been reached, however, most juniors will be keen to do some jumping, and they should be encouraged, for their riding will normally benefit from the experience even if their dominant interest remains one of the specialized forms of flat riding.

It is convenient to subdivide the rider's training over fences into three different phases, or levels, each characterized primarily by a different "release" of the horse's mouth during the approach. The lower the level, the earlier this release should take place, and the more certain should be the "insurance measures" the rider takes in order to obviate any possibility of grabbing the horse in the mouth with his hands.

# 6
# Jumping First Level

## POSTING WITH THE MOTION

Visualize a rider who is posting with the motion at the trot. His upper body angulation duplicates the rider's jumping and galloping positions. Because of its thrust of the upper body, the posting trot necessitates a forward inclination in order to remain in balance and not be left behind, and, correspondingly, as soon as the rider is able to post with the motion, he is ready to learn principles of jumping fences. Remember, and do not forget, that during all this elementary work the pupil must be forward about thirty degrees inside of the perpendicular.

The very first exercise in actually dealing with obstacles should focus on posting with the motion around the ring over an imaginary rail lying between a standard and the ring wall or between a pair of wings—anything that will form a chute, guiding the horse and keeping him straight. Once the rider is retaining his basic position around the ring at the trot, the imaginary rail should be replaced by a real rail lying on the ground, and the same demands imposed—trotting with the motion and holding onto a decent basic position.

### RELEASE (MANE)

The most important single factor in jumping an actual fence is the release of the horse's mouth on approaching the obstacle. Like any other exercise, this one should be learned first at a standstill and then practiced over a rail on the ground. Not only does this release allow a horse to increase his pace, but it also allows him use of his head and neck in flight over an obstacle. This basic principle is so much the most important first step in actually negotiating a jump that without its proper use and understanding no further progress can be made. When a beginner is taught this primary, or "first-step," release, he should be encouraged to take hold of the mane halfway up the horse's crest, holding the mane until the jump is completed, several strides on the other side. We call this a long release. This instills the principle into the rider from the beginning: Do not interfere with your horse's mouth at take-off, during the jump, or upon landing. Your release must be on the crest of the neck, as the crest provides maximum support. Riders releasing below the crest usually collapse with their hands and body upon landing over the fence, and those whose release is above this point interfere with the horse going over the jump.

Grabbing the mane is a technique in itself, and there are several different ways to do it; all should be practiced. The first and easiest is for both hands to reach up and simply grab it. Holding the mane in one hand and the reins in the other has the dual control advantage both of the horse's pace and using the neck as a support. A third way, one that I highly recommend, is for the rider to release his horse halfway up the crest with his inside hand only. This frees his outside hand to guide the horse along the ring fence, and, looking ahead toward exercises of more advanced nature, the pupil will need only to remove one hand from the horse's neck rather than two when learning to jump "out of hand." So, here are three technically correct ways of grabbing the mane, a release so basic and often unpracticed that many advanced riders have never done it, nor are they able to without a little practice. Do not fall prey to the myth that it is wrong to grab the mane; it is not. And, at very elementary stages, when dealing with either a novice or a green horse, it should be mandatory. At this stage, the maxim "Either the mane or the mouth" can hardly be refuted. It is a shame more riders do not heed it. Many a refusal or sticky jump is the direct result of a horse intimidated by having his mouth hit while in the air.

USING THE EYES

The next step toward security and balance over a jump is the rider's conscious control of his eyes. Eye control is just as important as that of hand, leg, or upper body. Most people somehow are made aware of release through knowing that the horse has got to be free enough in his head and neck at least to jump the jump; very few, though, realize the importance of looking ahead of themselves for the sake of balance as well as anticipation. This, therefore, I would consider the most common failing among groups of riders in general. And it is something that can be easily corrected and learned through simple drill exercises.

There are three steps in using the eyes to ride a line over a jump. The first is to search for the line before turning toward the jump or allowing the pace to increase for the jump. The next would be to ride the jump, or series of jumps, by looking ahead at a specific focal point over and beyond the last jump. The third step stops the horse squarely at the very end of the line, making sure that he stands still for a few seconds before going on to the next job. This last particular phase I label "finishing a job." During this and all other eye exercises, the only concern on the rider's part is to concentrate on looking ahead at the next jump or over his line of jumps, whichever the case may be.

There are many more advanced exercises connected with eye control that will help the rider become more and more independent of his natural inclination to look down. Using the instructor as a focal point and following this focal point as it moves in front of the jump to the side and even behind it are excellent exercises giving the rider the security and balance necessary. As soon as the eyes become totally independent, control is on the way. Also, one's reaction span is sharpened through these exercises.

HEELS AND LEGS

Depth of heel and proper leg position are next in importance for basic jumping technique. Without enough weight in the heel, the rider is bound to be jarred and jolted when landing after a fence. This flexed ankle acts as a shock absorber and cushion, and it is useful as a brace against horses that pull or bore. Definitely one of my quickest references to a rider's strength and security lies in an analysis of his leg position. Some riders of unusual athletic abilities do get away with faulty legs, which, however, is never a sound criterion by which to judge or teach. The average student can never be expected to compensate for unusual form with the exceptional balance, feeling, or timing possessed by the occasional rider of gifted dimension, and it is very unfair to expect him to follow the rider of unorthodox style as a learning example.

It must be explained that holding the leg just behind the back edge of the girth is vital in relation to the upper body position. Only when the upper body is held over and not behind the leg can it be with the motion of the horse. As soon as the leg comes forward in front of the body the rider must throw himself in order to catch up with his horse over the jump. The same holds true when posting behind the motion; it is a lot more work. Contrarily, the leg placed too far back is no support to the upper body, which topples forward ahead of the motion. That is why riders whose legs are forward are behind their horse and, though they are not often smooth, do many times prove effective. But the rider whose legs are too far back never rides well. Being with the motion is correct and being behind the motion can be useful; but being ahead of the motion is completely useless. Therefore, learn to hold the correct leg position from the very beginning.

SEQUENCE OF OBSTACLES

Acquainting a rider with the motion of jumping a fence becomes a very simple and gradual sequence. The first jump a rider should be asked to take, perhaps at a very early stage of riding, is an imaginary fence. This "jump" does not necessarily need wings, i.e., rails or wooden frames used to keep the horse from running out. I am not a great advocate of wings and only use them with a beginner or when absolutely necessary. They tend to provide a psychological crutch which once impressed on the rider's mind sometimes becomes hard to erase. Wings are not necessary if the training of horse and rider is proper. In practicing this first jumping exercise, the rider should be asked to post with the motion to and over his imaginary jump, looking ahead at a focal point at the end of the ring. He should release the horse by grabbing the mane about three strides ahead of the jump while keeping his heels down.

Good teaching demands that each one of the jumping prerequisites be isolated and practiced over and over before the next step is undertaken. However, after one full lesson over an imaginary jump, the rider, even the most elementary, is ready to trot over a rail lying on the ground. It is best to keep this work, too, at a trot, not only because of the safety of the slower gait but also because the rider must be in a correct forward jumping position if he is posting with the motion. Remember that at the posting trot, the hand gallop, and while approaching a jump, the upper body must be inclined forward so that the rider's and horse's centers of gravity correspond, one in line with the other. Riding behind the motion into a jump (using the cantering position, deep in the saddle) is something more advanced which will be discussed later.

The six-inch-high cross rail provides the next logical step and lets the rider really feel the horse jump; most horses will hop off the ground at a cross rail. It is most important, now that the horse is actually leaving the ground, for the instructor to be sure the rider releases the animal's mouth and is grabbing the mane halfway up the crest. Continue to stress the rider's keeping his eyes up and fixed upon a point above and beyond the jump, as this is the only way he can feel his form and faults. Before attempting another step in height, a straight rail about a foot off the ground, check that the heels remain driven down and the legs held in position over the low cross rail. It is easy to jump higher; it takes time and practice to jump better.

## UPPER BODY CONTROL—TWO- AND THREE-POINT CONTACT

If the rider is jumping a small rail with an automatic release before his jump, his eyes up, and so forth, he is ready to concentrate on upper body control. This can only be learned in the two-point contact position, the rider standing in his stirrups and a little out of the saddle, the contact with the horse being only between his two legs and not with his seat at all. In practice, as he approaches the jump, the rider stands in his two-point position, waiting for the horse's thrust to close up the body angle at the joint of thigh and upper body. He does not think "jump" nor throw his body at the horse, which would unsettle a sensitive animal and is unnecessary excess motion. Consequently, the rider in this light position is already with his horse and does not feel urged to throw himself forward in order to catch up in the air. It is for this very reason that smoothing out a rider's performance in regard to his upper body must be learned in two-point contact.

One of the most common, most unnecessary, and most harmful habits is that of the rider "ducking" over fences. The prime characteristic of a ducker is his dropping his head down below the horse's crest, producing far more motion than is necessary. The actual duck, in itself, can never be directly attacked at first, there being two basic underlying faults creating the habit. As a rule, the rider's leg position is too far forward, causing the rider to have to throw his upper body in order to catch up with his horse in the air because he had been behind the motion approaching the fence. Of course, if one comes to the jump too deep in the saddle even with a proper leg position, the most athletic horseman will be forced into throwing his trunk forward at take-off.

While ducking can be most detrimental to a performance, especially when sensitive, quick horses are ridden, the rider who perches ahead of his horse with his leg too far back is committing a far more serious error, losing both control and security. Always remember that one can function either with or behind the motion of his horse, but never ahead of it. As soon as a horse is in the position to fall behind his pilot, anything and everything can go wrong—and usually does! We must always examine the rider's leg position first and control his base of support and upper body angulation second. Nothing can be corrected without lower leg control, especially the body's balance and weight displacement. I'm sure you've seen good riders possessed of a correct leg position or strong capable horsemen with their legs too far forward, but when have you seen anyone ride well with their legs too far back?

Another habit with potentially severe consequences is that of dropping back too early in the air. Almost without exception, like ducking, it is seen in riders who ride behind their horse's motion with their legs too far forward. This causes a throwing forward motion as the horse leaves the ground and then the reverse reaction during descent. Obviously if the fault is carried to excess, especially when jumping bigger fences, it will inhibit and even prohibit animals from using their hind legs to their fullest advantage. To my mind, the rider's hand and weight should be as passive and quiet as possible from the moment of take-off until landing, presenting no interference during this period of suspension. Not only should the horse's physical apparatus be left to its own devices while air-borne, but, more important, his concentration should be undistracted from the job at hand, which is jumping the jump. While many people, myself included, feel that for a performance of a consistent and sophisticated nature the strides be controlled to the take-off point, relatively few believe in passivity in the air. With the exception of counteracting dwelling or rushing during suspension, there is really nothing the rider can do except to allow the horse his freedom, both mentally and physically, to take the jump. For this reason, dropping back in the air must be considered a serious fault worthy of correction. As I said before, the correction lies first and foremost in seeing that the lower leg is well placed just behind the girth. Then to make things easier and a bit more prearranged, have the pupil assume his two-point contact stance, insisting that he hold it throughout the different phases of the jump and only coming back in the saddle at the end of his line.

Only after smoothness and security are achieved should the rider learn to approach the jump in three-point contact, with light seat contact in the saddle. Actually, as we said earlier, there are two kinds of three-point contact: crotch contact and buttock contact. When in a crotch position, the rider's upper body is forward, his hip angle is closed, yet he is deep in his saddle. While in a buttock seat, the upper body is erect, the hip angle is open, and he is very deep in the saddle. The advantage of riding in three-point contact is that the rider remains deeper in his horse, thus keeping him more collected and balanced until take-off, with more weight distributed toward the rear. This position is also an aid in driving the horse forward, especially a hesitant, green horse, a balky refuser, or an open jumper needing the ultimate in balance for negotiating large obstacles.

Remember that a polished hunter round, galloping cross-country, or an equitation performance should be ridden predominantly in two-point contact on straight lines and in three-point crotch contact on turns. A very green horse, a rough rogue, or an open jumper should be ridden with a three-point buttock contact, as should any horse when jumping an especially difficult cross-country obstacle. Two-point position insures smooth, invisible riding, while three-point contributes to good balance and maximum control. In other words, the more the rider need control the horse in a difficult situation, the more he needs to stay "behind" his horse.

# 7
# *Jumping Second Level*

RELEASE (CREST)

The principal difference between first and second level jumping
has to do with release. You will remember that beginners should
grab the mane halfway up the horse's crest in the primary stages
of learning to jump, enabling them to get a well-grounded start
even before they've developed a sufficiently secure, independent
leg or seat. Now that the pupil has reached a secondary level,
however, and has a steady enough leg to prevent his being jarred
loose, he is ready to advance to the next stage of release.

There are two major differences between these two forms of
release. Of primary importance is that the second release takes
place during the last stride or two before the take-off point for
the jump, whereas the first mane-grabbing release took place
three or four strides in front of the obstacle during the approach. The other important difference is that the hands now
rest firmly on top of the crest of the horse's neck instead of grabbing the mane. Obviously this kind of support is much more independent than grabbing and holding onto the mane; moreover,
it is the introductory step toward asking the rider to jump "out
of hand," the release in which the horse's mouth is followed
during flight and no hand support at all is needed.

As in establishing any other body control habit, it is best to
teach and demonstrate this release of resting the hands a third of

the way up the crest at a standstill and then a walk, rather than first attempting it into a jump. Approaching any exercise slowly and in sequence not only makes it more understandable to the pupil, but also enhances his chances of feeling how to do it correctly. Something else to be noted at this time is spontaneous reaction, which can be practiced and improved by having the instructor ask the pupil to "rest" or "release" on command or to stand in front of the jump so the pupil may release his horse at a given visual signal, such as the dropping of the instructor's hand.

Now we teach two kinds of crest release: long and short. The long crest release, as we taught the beginner, moves anywhere from a third to halfway up the horse's crest. This insures maximum freedom for the horse and minimum control for the rider during the flight of the jump. The short crest release, on the other hand, maximizes control and minimizes freedom, although the horse should not hit the bit while in the air. While the long crest release rests up the horse's crest, the short release rests down and into the base of the crest, an inch or two up from the withers.

### CO-ORDINATING THE RELEASE AND LEG

The intermediate jumping rider's next concern is to practice the co-ordination of his driving aids with the release of his hand. We'll first take the driving leg into consideration as this is the one most commonly used and consistently needed. It's convenient to compare the action of the legs with that of an automobile gas pedal and the hands with a car's brakes. A driver doesn't put his foot on the gas until he's released the brake; a rider should, likewise, first be taught only to apply leg pressure after releasing his horse's mouth. This specific co-ordination sequence —release followed by leg application on the approach to a jump —can soon be reversed, teaching the rider to apply first a leg and

89. *Good classic form.* Though not possessed of great length of leg, Miss Kristine Pfister, shown here aboard her famous Valhalla, demonstrates how it should be done through sheer determination and brilliant timing. The strength of purpose is apparent in her expression. Here also is an excellent demonstration of a short crest release.

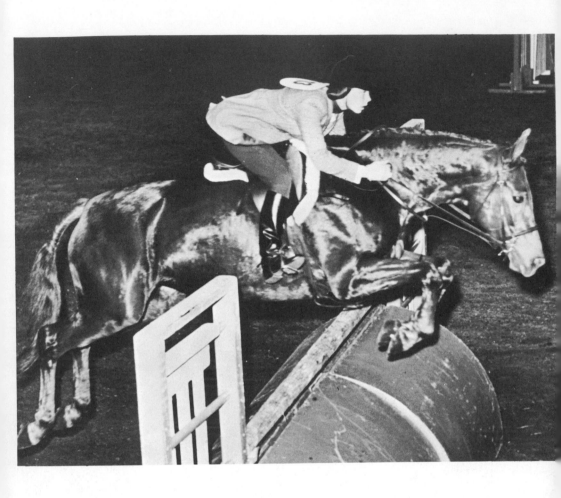

90. *Good classic form.* Short in height, Miss Jen Marsden has to situate herself quite behind a horse at all times to use what length she has to best advantage. This, however, in no way hinders her definite approach to riding; and with her terrific "eye for a distance" she may be an inspiration to those who think they're not built to ride. Note the automatic release, or what's called jumping "out of hand"—a straight line from horse's mouth to rider's elbow. PHOTO BY FREUDY

91. *Good classic form.* While Miss Susan Bauer's reins might be a trifle short, her gift for tact and poise on her flighty junior jumper Sneeze clearly comes through. More intellectual than instinctive as a rider, Sue (now Mrs. Ronnie Mutch) represents the epitome in studied presence. PHOTO BY FREUDY

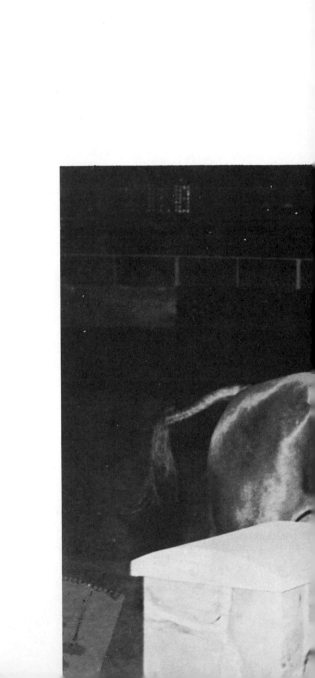

92. *Good classic form.* Elasticity, softness, and sympathy characterize Conrad Homfeld's style. Every horse he rides seems to flow freely forward, never having to fight his delicate hand. While I don't like the thumb up, notice the light hand-rein-mouth relationship. Since this photo was taken, Conrad has become one of the great international jumping riders of the world, often representing our USET.

93. *Good classic form.* Finesse is the word best used to describe Miss Brooke Hodgson on her mare Scotch Tweed. Never one for a fight, Brooke handles the most touchy situations and comes out ahead. While I don't advocate opening the fingers, Brooke's trademark as a rider is refinement right down to her finger tips. PHOTO BY BUDD

94. *Good classic form.* Comprehensive nerve and a "go for broke" attitude are admirable traits. Miss Kip Rosenthal displays both here as she rides her versatile Rome Dome. Notice how correctly she regulates her four major riding angles—ankle, knee, hip, and elbow. Due to the fact that Kip had to work to learn to ride, she now has become an excellent teacher. PHOTO BY GEORGE AXT

95. *Riding an outside course with the motion.* The basic position used in showing a hunter regardless of how badly the horse is carrying himself. The rider is out of the saddle a bit and using her hands low over the withers below the horse's mouth so as not emphasize the high head carriage.

96. *Riding an outside course behind the motion.* One should ride a gallop in the saddle only during situations requiring additional drive, such as with very green horses and stoppers or when approaching exceptionally tricky obstacles.

97. *The reality of the elbow-hand-mouth relationship in the air*. Very often it would be impossible, as here, to follow the horse's mouth in the air and stay in line without the collapse of the upper body. Rather than have the hands somewhere down around the shoulders, I much prefer the following of the crest.

98. *A workmanlike expression*. This girl's whole riding attitude shows in her face. By concentrating straight ahead, she is absolutely relaxed and in command of her work. This is the mental self-control we want to achieve.

99. *Two riders well turned out before entering the ring*. Both horse and rider should be immaculately groomed and well turned out before being asked to perform in public.

100. *A good example of hunter riding*. Freedom and lightness of hand and seat were why bold, strong horses like Pike's Pcak went softly and kindly for Mrs. Joan Walsh Hogan. Her "equestrian tact" was unsurpassed. Nowadays, of course, riding with the stirrup home is rarely seen in the show ring; we prefer to keep it on the ball of the foot. CARL KLEIN PHOTO

101. *Riding an appointment class.* While Rodney Jenkins' style is not rigidly classic in that his heel might slip a bit in the air or his back might be loose, very few riders ever approach his instinctive understanding of a horse or his fantastic "eye" for a fence. In light of the fact that Rodney rides so many different horses so well week after week, we might say he has been the greatest horseman of our times. PHOTO BY P. A. GORMUS, JR., COURTESY THE RICHMOND TIMES-DISPATCH AND NEWS LEADER

102. *Negotiating a puissance wall.* Miss Kathy Kusner's trust in a horse's jumping mechanism in the air is why she can get more out of most horses than other riders who try to "help." Notice her absolutely independent hand and leg while jumping Untouchable over seven feet. PHOTO BY JEAN BRIDEL, L'ANNÉE HIPPI-QUE, LAUSANNE

103. *Riding a jumper with style.* There are very few classicists in stadium jumping today. Mrs. Mary Mairs Chapot is certainly one of them and here, on White Lightning, she is exhibiting "picture book" form over a rather large Aachen oxer. Due to Mary's riding experience and to being a stylist, she is now one of our very best equitation judges. PHOTO BY UDO SCHMIDT

104. *Riding a jumper with strength.* Frank Chapot's mental determination combined with great physical strength make him one of the most aggressive riders I've ever seen. Frank's expression here clearly indicates his attitude towards Diamant and this oxer. Frank not only continues to ride well but is also one of our top judges and course designers. PHOTO BY MITSCHKE, WIESBADEN

105. *The author riding.* It was hard to look too bad on Sinjon no matter what, although I wish my elbows were closer to my body. I guess I'll never change: I'll always worry first about the rider's style and technique before putting too much blame on the horse. Perhaps that is why I love my work, teaching, so very, very much. PHOTO BY THEODOR JANSSEN

then release. In this way, he is putting his horse to the bit before taking the jump, which again is a step toward jumping "out of hand." Such exercises as isolating and controlling the particular use of the hand and the leg coming into a jump prove invaluable later on when dealing with horses of varying temperaments. Some horses—usually hot, sensitive animals—jump better from just the allowance of the hand and no leg at all. A more moderate temperament requires a bit of leg support in conjunction with easing off the mouth; and a sluggish beast is in need of spurs to enforce an already strong leg. Of course, these differences must be felt in degrees.

USING THE CLUCK

After a bit of practice in co-ordinating the release and leg, it comes time to introduce two more driving aids used in place of or in addition to the squeezing leg. The first and simplest to master is the use of the cluck, which is brought into focus at a standstill while the rider is shown its application used simultaneously with the stick behind the saddle. That is, in essence, how the horse is educated to the cluck. Only by associating the stick with the cluck will the horse learn to respond to the noise by itself. The action of the cluck should move the horse from a standstill right up onto the bit; and if he doesn't move quickly enough to the bit, the rider must again hold him still, applying his voice and his stick at the same time until the horse responds solely to the voice aid.

As we've said, the cluck replaces or accents the action of the leg. This statement can be a bit misleading. Only on rare occasions, usually with the touchy mare who can't tolerate leg pressure, does the voice work all by itself independently of other aids. More times than not its great advantage is that of a leg accent and nothing more. This is quite unlike the stick which, by itself, is a very powerful driving aid. More of a request than a demand, the cluck should be utilized when just a little more driving force is needed, encouraging the horse to move forward or leave the ground.

The actual sequence and co-ordination of this invaluable aid naturally can and should be discussed and practiced as a follow-up to the leg on the flat before it is incorporated into the jumping technique. For instance, if the rider asks for a canter depart and the horse is reluctant to move from leg aid alone, a cluck may be incorporated, getting the desired result. Be very careful, however, that the rider understands he is to cluck only once or twice clearly and not to continue clucking if no response is forthcoming. If the animal doesn't react to one or two clucks, the rider must stop requesting and start demanding, or, in other words, use his stick! No rider could exhibit a weaker habit than that of repeatedly clucking while going around the ring or coming into a jump. Not only is the rider not getting the desired result, but at the same time his horse quickly acquires disrespect and disregard for the aid itself.

Now that the rider has understood and applied the cluck on the flat, it will be easy for him to duplicate its purpose approaching a jump. Unlike the leg, which gradually squeezes the horse into the take-off zone, the cluck quickly and momentarily evokes a forward response. My particular drill practice for incorporating this aid into the pupil's technique requires the use of the cluck three or four strides away from the jump on approach, at the take-off point, or during flight through the air. By doing this the rider will consciously know how to counteract a hesitant approach into the fence, a "sticky" take-off, or a horse that dwells in the air. I've rarely found it necessary to teach driving aids upon landing after a jump, provided the approach, take-off, and flight are properly directed. Be ready, though, for the exception to this rule does arise in rare instances. Let me repeat again about the number of clucks: one or two only, or else the rider starts sounding like a parrot, and a weak one at that!

## USING THE STICK

The use of the stick and that of the cluck, though closely related, should be thought of as sharply different degrees of punishment for similar disobediences. For the beginner and intermediate, the most important thing to know about a stick is how to use it and when! In one of the preceding sections we've outlined steps for using the stick correctly. We'll repeat: Take the reins in one hand, forming a bridge, reach back of the saddle (not on the horse's shoulder), and hit the horse on the flank; return immediately to the reins with both hands. A common fault often seen is to turn the stick over in the hand before using it. Instead of punishing the horse, the rider is then in the position to beat him, which usually happens, causing a scared animal rather than an educated one. Another point to remember is always to carry a stick in your more dexterous hand, be it right or left. (Of course there are always exceptions to the rule, such as with a horse that always runs out at a jump to a particular side or drifts to one corner or the other.)

After having practiced the same drill exercise on the flat (following up the leg by use of the stick) as the rider did with the cluck, he is ready to go into his jumping work with a stick as a useful aid rather than just a prop. Both the stick and the cluck are used in exactly the same ways and at the same times, although the former is a bit more difficult to master since more co-ordination is required. Also, horses tend to increase their pace a bit from a stick, which inhibits the more timid souls; and when the rider is using a stick on approaching a fence, the horse has more time to run out unless the rider is quick to return to both reins.

As far as timing the stick with the correct take-off point, the rider, as his "eye for distance" becomes established, will automatically hit the horse at the right spot. It's a great mistake to clutter the rider's mind by worrying him to death about "timing" the stick. It satisfies completely at this stage of the game that he do it at approximately the right time.

To practice stick application during the flight of the jump while the horse is air-borne is very important; it is the only way of correcting a horse that dwells or hesitates in the air, a very serious fault when going into advanced work over larger courses.

Before we go on, it should be learned that there is a great deal of difference between educating a horse to a strange or difficult obstacle and just plain showing him the jump. I, for one, am a great believer in conditioning a horse to jump anything he's faced at the very first time as well as possible without any major hesitations. For this reason, I've found it risky to allow horses to examine fences before jumping them, which tends to make them always want to look first and jump afterward. By walking a horse up to a suspicious obstacle and applying a driving aid, be it spurs, a cluck, or, as in this instance, a stick back of the saddle, the horse is quickly conditioned to think forward when going to jump that obstacle. In a sense, by walking to the jump and pulling up we've committed a refusal. We then punish that refusal, making clear our forward intention. In other words, we have created a disobedience in order to have an excuse for a corrective punishment.

## LINES AND TURNS

One discipline I've found most important, especially at this crucial level of making a rider, is what I call "holding a line." In actuality, no jump or line of jumps is ever negotiated without having previously been planned, either consciously or unconsciously, on a line. Even in jumping off very tight turns, some sort of line is established, sometimes as late as the take-off point. Of course, when I talk of "establishing a line" I don't mean to insinuate that all jumps are jumped at right angles for they by no means are. I am simply implying that all jumps are lined up in the rider's mind and eye with a start, middle, and end, whether jumping perpendicular to the fence or on acute angles. It is obvious, therefore, that the basic line work done at the beginner level, that of establishing, riding out, and stopping smoothly on a line, must be continually and forever repeated lest sloppy approaches and finishes start cropping up in an otherwise disciplined performance. By the way, one of the surest, quickest ways of preventing horses from cutting their corners either before or after a line of jumps, is to practice this straight line work with exactness, allowing not even a foot or two of deviation.

Turns, our next object of concentration, are really incorporated into our line work, and good turns aren't possible without a previous understanding and control of disciplined line riding. To give an example of perhaps the most basic turn into a jump, the rider establishes his trotting or cantering pace at one end of the ring while his eyes search out his line of jumps or single jump, as the case may be. As he approaches his line, he starts turning toward his first fence, all the time concentrating on nothing but his own eye control. Upon completion of his line of jumps, he rides straight to the end of the ring and makes a turn, retaining the same pace. In other words, the rider is still finishing his line but continues on at the same pace rather than stopping at his termination point. In this way, a feeling of continuity can be achieved, combining lines and turns, which is really all that riding a course of jumps consists of.

A very good exercise, again providing continuity of pace and requiring only one or two fences, incorporates the line followed by a half-turn or a half-turn in reverse, returning over the original fences in the opposite direction, followed by a stop. Of course, in order to elongate the exercise, the turns may be repeated five or six times in order to provide a multiseries of lines, jumps, and turns.

Of all problems encountered in turning, as in stopping, lightness and balance remain the most prominent. Horses, for the most part, tend to be too heavy on their forehands to be able to make light, agile turns. This is due to a great extent to the rider's weight being an added, unnatural burden; therefore, it is up to the rider and his influences to help a horse regain his balance after galloping and jumping so that he can negotiate the turns. Animals that cannot turn lightly and in balance cannot be considered under complete control and consequently are bound to approach their next line of fences in a haphazard manner.

The most important physical change required of a rider making a turn is to open up (straighten up) his upper body and to sink softly into the saddle. His mass (weight) will then be more centrally located, making it easier for the horse to shift his own center of gravity from his shoulders toward his quarters. Be careful, though, not to overdo this change of upper body angulation; ten or fifteen degrees is plenty and any more than that is rough, excess motion which is completely unnecessary.

Along with changing his weight distribution, the rider uses his hands to steady the horse by closing, and if necessary, raising them a shade. Of course, the heavier the horse is on his forehand, the more the rider will be forced to lighten him up by raising his head and neck. Always remember that the hand action must be accompanied by depressing the heels more, so that the leg doesn't slip too far back around the turn, thus losing its irreplaceable strength as a brace against any pulling or leaning on the horse's part.

## COMBINATIONS

All the previous exercises may be incorporated into work over combinations. It is best to start the pupil over a single in-and-out (two jumps close together) approximately twenty-four feet apart. This is a very straightforward, normal, and nice distance for the average horse at a slow jumping gallop; and it's really unnecessary to complicate or add to this combination for a little while as there are many drill exercises to be performed over these two simple jumps. A jump is considered part of a combination if it is within thirty-nine feet six inches of another jump. If they are any farther apart, they are considered separate fences.

Of primary psychological as well as actual importance is making the intermediate rider realize that the first jump of any combination is the crucial one and any other fence or fences following almost take care of themselves. Technically, if we use our basic one-stride in-and-out, success should and will be achieved through pace control and a cluck for take-off. By increasing his pace just a little bit and utilizing the forward reaction produced by the cluck for the first part of the combination, the rider will have no difficulty in jumping longer in-and-outs which he'll be encountering over a low outside course. Personally, I feel it is more important to teach the rider how to lengthen a horse's stride and jump off this long stride, than to show him how to shorten up, and by having the cluck at hand he will associate boldness and aggressiveness with combinations.

Now that the rider has learned to demand and obtain a one-stride in-and-out, it is his job to return to concentrating on smoothness and polish. All during this level of riding the rider's release remains relatively long up the horse's crest for the duration of the whole combination; and his heels must be carefully watched too, to see that they don't slip up.

Presuming that the three basic jumping "musts" have been given some time to be absorbed and made permanent, much of the rider's attention should now focus on upper body control. Combinations offer great opportunity for split-second weight distribution, which we have previously divided into two, and three-point contact. The control differential between staying off a horse's back or, on the contrary, being able to sink down into the back during the phases of approach or landing is clearly seen during combination work. For example, as an exercise I'll have the pupil assume his two-point galloping position (crotch out of the saddle) and approach the combination. He'll jump the combination's first element without coming back into the saddle; then he'll jump the second element, land, and smoothly sink back into his full seat. Next, the rider should be asked to approach the combination in a three-point contact, hold his two-point position between the two fences, and only resume his full seat after the second fence. Any possible variations of the two- and three-point contact exercises must lead to quick reactions when weight distribution will be needed in order to exert full restraint or drive.

In short, combinations at this level are important not for their own sake but rather as reinforcement exercises for habits already begun over simple single fences. Those specific problems encountered when riding series of fences separated by variable distances will be thoroughly explored during a later, more advanced riding stage. Rider and teacher alike must never lose sight of the fact that now is the time to develop and enforce form and technique, not after a rider has built an incorrect foundation and style yet still rides effectively well. It is true that old habits are hard to change; and this is especially so if poor form is maintained by a talented rider who had tasted success because of nerve and timing. Psychologically, this type of person finds it hard to believe that he not only would look better through proper, slow training, but that he could also produce more effectively. It is all a matter of acceptance: those who want to change for the better can, no matter how many blue ribbons they've won riding in bad form.

## ANGLES

By the time angle fences are introduced into a rider's schooling work, his release is ready to be modified. Up until now we've been releasing a third to halfway up the horse's crest, thereby allowing maximum freedom. Jumping fences on an angle automatically inhibits such abandonment because of the fact that run-outs are bound to occur unless light contact and guidance are maintained. For this very reason the pupil will use a short release or learn to jump his horse out of hand, maintaining constant contact and control over the horse's mouth out of necessity imposed by the angulation during both the approach and the flight of the jump. I've found this, personally, to be the most natural, unconscious approach in teaching a rider to "jump out of hand," a phrase often used, more often abused, and rarely accomplished correctly. The term "out of hand" simply means that the rider controls each stride right up to the take-off point, maintaining light contact with the mouth in the air and resuming control of the strides upon landing.

Along with more of a contact hand-mouth relationship, the rider, while jumping angle fences, is forced into being more exact with his eyes. Plans of lines thought out ahead of time can't be too specific for angling effectively and smoothly. Interestingly enough, I've found angulation control to be one of the most determining factors in a rider's transition from intermediate to advanced levels.

To angle jumps successfully, the horse must be kept on the bit at all times and his pace decreased to lessen the chances of running out. If run-outs are encountered, especially with the young horse, come right back to the slow sitting trot if necessary. Specific angulations may be anywhere from slight to acute, the lesser approaching ninety degrees perpendicular to the jump and the more extreme angles being close to twenty degrees. Angling exercises of any kind are good for horse and rider alike. I do it a great deal with young horses over low fences as it is most helpful in teaching them to wait and not rush their jumps.

## APPROACHING A COURSE

Enough background, consisting mostly of repetitious drill exercises, has now been given to the intermediate rider. He may now begin to explore his ultimate goal—jumping a course. Again, as in all our other work, the course will be broken down and simplified, with the pupil practicing each part before attempting the whole.

The beginning of any course is the preparatory part, the circle. There are many approaches to this circle and many reasons for exercising different controls during its execution in preparation for the first fence. However, for the moment we aren't involved with complicated, sophisticated riding, but rather with a simple, smooth performance. It's been my experience that the simplest, smoothest, and yet most controlled circle upon entering a ring incorporates three different gaits. The posting trot, the slow sitting trot, and the canter, in that sequence.

Entering the ring, the rider posts at an ordinary eight-mile-an-hour trot; approaching the ring rail, he brings his horse back to a slow six-mile-an-hour sitting trot to insure collection, whereupon he applies his aids and puts his horse into a canter. As soon as the canter has been picked up, the rider, in his galloping position, concentrates immediately on establishing the set pace he wants to maintain for the duration of the particular course to be jumped. Remember, an equitation and any hunter performance is judged on smoothness and evenness of pace from beginning to end! It's certainly not the time, and it's much too late, to pick a pace after the second fence has been jumped.

An elementary ring course designed for the intermediate should be composed primarily of lines and turns, with an occasional combination and angle fence thrown in. In other words, try to incorporate naturally, easily, and in sequence all the exercises the rider has so far encountered. Attempting a course of excessive difficulty at this stage will only tend to distract the rider from his technical concentration. Smooth, proper technique is all that should be demanded now, and the fences need be no higher than two and a half or three feet at the very most.

As in all other work, it is so much easier learning when only one thing is asked at a time. Therefore, riding a course of jumps should be divided up into perhaps five parts, the first of which is preparation before entering the ring.

Preparation always must be directly concerned with the horse's temperament. For the strong, keen horse, working on a circle trotting and stopping would be the best exercise, softening him up and making him wait and listen to the hand. A good approach for the horse who is sluggish and apt to be "sticky" over his fences is to hold him at the in-gate and before entering the ring to reach back and apply a stick along with a cluck. This last preparation is a sure-fire way of producing quick animation and response to the leg, for upon entering the ring for a competitive performance, the horse must be ready to move instantly from the leg, yet attentively alert to the hand. In other words, the horse must be between the rider's legs and up into his hands at all times if the rider expects a good percentage of winning rounds.

The next segment of our course, following pre-entrance ring preparation, is, of course, the circle approaching the first fence. This circle is the only place where the rider can make a transition from the previous preparation to the actual course of jumps. Immediate attention on the horse's part must be established along with prompt transitions between the three basic gaits described—the posting trot, slow trot, and canter. The very moment the rider has taken up the canter he must set forth to increase his speed to his horse's best-suited pace for the particular course.

Now we're left with the remainder, the course itself, which is easiest to divide up approximately into thirds—beginning fences, middle fences, and the last fences which includes a smooth, relaxed finish. These groups of fences should be worked on for a time before putting them all together into one course complete with turns, changes of direction, etc. Specific lines and specific paces for those lines are all that really matter. Remember, too, that during all course work the rider's attention should rest solely on his eyes and on controlling his horse's speed. Nothing more should complicate the already difficult problem of negotiating a whole series of jumps and turns and lines; this rather too-simple principle holds true most of the time no matter how sophisticated the level of riding practiced. It is best not to overburden the rider's mind, especially during competition. Any problem related to form or technique should be noted and worked on over simple drill fences during the next lesson or session. Habits are developed slowly and individually, not all at once!

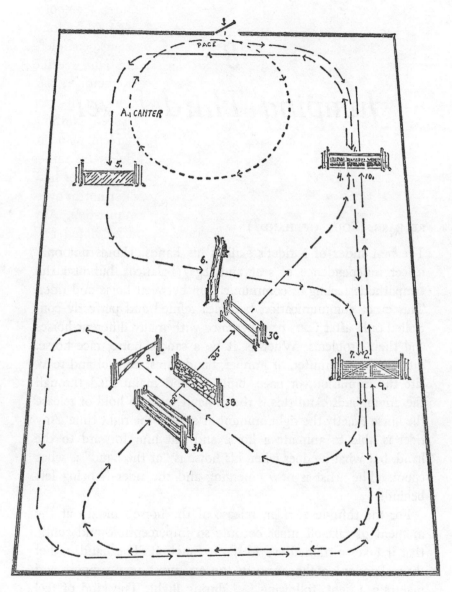

20. An equitation course

# 8

# Jumping Third Level

RELEASE ("OUT OF HAND")

The best index of a rider's skill is his hands. Hands not only reflect independence of seat and legs (balance) but also the sympathetic feeling of communication between horse and rider. This exact communication becomes refined and perfectly controlled only after years of experience with many different horses and their problems. Whether it be a saddle horse, race horse, dressage horse, hunter, or jumper, hands must control and regulate the impulsion, or pace, built up and maintained through the driving aids. And this is the difficult task: to hold or release the horse exactly the right amount at exactly the right time! Any rider is able to animate a horse and put him forward to the hand, but what he does when his horse is "at the hand" is what counts. The artist is now emerging and the rider is being left behind!

For the third-level rider, release of the horse's mouth at the moment of take-off must become so imperceptible and subtle that it takes a trained eye to see it function. The hand, rather than abandoning the horse in the air, must now support and maintain a light, following feel during flight. The kind of feel one describes as a "feathery touch." If there is any sign of the hands rotating backward or relying on the mouth for balance and support, then the rider is not secure enough or experienced enough to move on to this third advanced stage of release. The hand should *never* rely on the mouth for support, whereas the horse's mouth often relies on the rider's hand for support and balance.

Of all jumping faults, rotating the hands backward is the most serious simply because the horse isn't given enough freedom of head and neck to do his job. It doesn't take even the boldest animal long when trying to work under this rider's hand to associate jumping with mouth punishment. And if we review reward and punishment we can see why "stoppers" are usually ridden by riders who don't give their horses enough head. Whenever horses are stopping, the first thing to be considered is how the rider's hand is working. Under no conditions should severe driving aids be administered without making sure that the horse will be completely free to go forward in front of these aids.

My approach to teaching a rider to jump with a completely independent hand (jumping out of hand) employs a variety of exercises without reins (and often without stirrups) through multiple in-and-outs—a series of rails about two feet high and between ten and twelve feet apart. By jumping this low series without hands (hands on hips, on the head, behind the back, outstretched, in front of the chest, etc.) over and over again, the different parts of the rider's body become independent of one another and have no need for the hands as support. When the rider takes up the reins, he will feel no need to rely on the mouth or the crest of the neck for support. In reality, however, I've found that the crest of the neck and even wisps of mane come in handy, at times, even for the experts. No matter how secure a rider may be, there are often irregularities of take-off or unusual situations during flight that force the rider to rely on the crest of the neck. In short, one must always aim at achieving an independent, unsupported release, but never at the expense of balancing on the horse's mouth—the worst jumping crime of all!

Another very good exercise to teach jumping "out of hand," or as we now label it, an automatic release, is for the instructor to stand at a focal point fifty to seventy-five feet in front of a low fence and hold up his right hand. As the rider reaches the take-off to the jump, the instructor drops his hand, and the pupil moves into a crest release. The point is to wait until the signal is given before moving into the release. At one point the instructor does not drop his hand, the rider does nothing with his hands to indicate moving into a release, and the automatic release should naturally take place.

## TOTAL POSITION

We are now at the most dangerous stage of a rider's progression. He is advanced in the realm of the average or the amateur, yet he has not reached the rarefied atmosphere of the artistic expert. This is the crucial stage. It is the time for constant review and the hour for discussion and more discussion, not a time for standstill. A rider will either continue working to reinforce his body position and technique or slip into bad habits and regress.

In short, the rider's technique may be observed and improved upon only by riding many, many different horses with many different problems at different levels of schooling. A strong rider is only strong if he is able to counteract any and all resistances the horse may put up *without* affecting the horse's temperament and nervous system. A rider who overpunishes and overrides I label a "butcher." A butcher always creates a nervous, tense, rigid animal and one who is not responsive to soft, subtle aids. A horse of this kind is never emotionally or physically free enough to work at his best or produce the most.

The jumping rider's position should now be clearly his own, yet always within a classical frame. His legs should remain steady at all times, working either together or one at a time. The ball of the foot should have no trouble in resting on the stirrup and the stirrup should rarely be lost. If the stirrup is lost, the rider, if he has worked a good percentage of the time (at least 25 per cent) without stirrups, should have no trouble completing the course. The two-point and three-point contact should be automatically assumed at the appropriate times with the hip angle closing because of the horse's thrust, not the rider's physical gyrations. There should be an absolute *minimum* use of the upper body, with eyes remaining up and looking far in advance of the horse's present position. The arms and hands should remain for the most part in line with the mouth, supple, steady, and straight, with the release coinciding with the take-off point of the fence. The use of the cluck, spurs, or stick should be instantaneous whenever the leg does not produce an immediate forward reaction.

All in all, the rider at this point should ride in form with strength of purpose, security, and smoothness. He should be able to obtain the desired result and accomplish the task at hand, with the least effort possible. A quiet, authoritative rider is a quiet, authoritative rider because his body has been trained to assume the best functioning position and because he has a comprehensive backlog of technique to resort to should any problem of resistance arise. There is no mystical secret to the polished "pretty" rider who obtains the best performance time after time. It is merely a question of understanding, practice, and belief in a systematic approach.

RIDING "WITH" VERSUS "BEHIND" THE MOTION

The rider's understanding and application of two- and three-point contact must now correspond to his being with or behind the motion of his horse. As has been stated, the term "with the motion" applies to the state of the rider's center of gravity being directly over the horse's center of gravity, while "behind the motion" places the rider's gravity behind that of the horse. Naturally, the farther behind the motion the rider gets, the better a position he is in to use his weight either as a "driving" or "holding" force. Weight, after all, is what really controls the horse's motor (his hind legs) after the hands and legs have been applied.

In principle, I believe that the hunter or equitation horse should be jumped in a light two-point and crotch three-point (with the motion) contact. I firmly believe in teaching this kind of riding first since a rider should ride hunters and, if possible, equitation before going on to the art of open jumping. Also, I've found it much easier for the good forward rider to learn to sit down and get behind his horse than it is for the good rider who has always been behind the motion to get out of the saddle and stay light. Naturally, if during a hunter or equitation round a serious hesitation does occur, the rider's correct natural instinct should be followed and he should open up (straighten up) his body, sink down in the saddle, and drive forward. On the other hand, in working and showing a horse for hunter or equitation purposes, there is no reason to compromise with a particular animal's strong, quick, tense temperament and sit down in the saddle to facilitate holding. Through the use of the hand in conjunction with the proper bit and martingale and along with a strongly driven down heel and tight knee and thigh, any horse may be regulated and held in this light forward seat. By performing with the motion, maximum smoothness is insured and a quiet, subtle performance displayed. Only when the rider appears to do nothing has *art* been achieved!

There are certain situations that are prearranged or happen to arise when it is imperative to sit down and stay behind one's horse—jumping trappy fences over difficult terrain, riding very green or balky horses, and negotiating large courses such as those in open jumper competition. By the rider's straightening up his body and displacing his weight more to the rear, the horse's forehand is lightened, which makes for a quicker, more agile use of this half of his body. As soon as the rider assumes this more vertical position, he is accepting the permanent role of balancer and dictator. In other words, he will already be in the position of ultimate strength and won't have to waste time getting there. Of course, when situations of great difficulty are known beforehand, the rider should remain behind the motion for the duration of the task, whether it be riding a Nation's Cup course or driving a balky horse across a stream.

Riding behind one's horse, as we've stated, is often much more effective under certain conditions; however, it can never be quite as smooth. As soon as the body approaches a fence behind the motion, it has a great deal further to go in order to be with the motion during flight. (Being behind the motion or ahead of it in the air is, for obvious reasons, always detrimental to the horse's freedom.) This additional distance makes it necessary for the rider as well as the horse's thrust to close the hip angle and catch up with the horse's arc. This naturally increases the upper body motion and is not as smooth as when with the motion. Usually people who have acquired the bad fault of "ducking" ride continually behind the motion and have learned to "get with" their horse in the air by throwing their body forward at the moment of take-off. This is a very serious fault as it tends to make a quick horse quicker and more apprehensive. Ducking is only corrected by a great deal of exaggerated two-point stance work.

## LINES, TURNS, COMBINATIONS, ANGLES

Exercising over simple lines will now be replaced, for the most part, by working over complicated segments of courses. These segments usually include not only lines but also turns, angles, and combinations. In other words, any series of problems requiring split-second control will now be used to quicken the rider's reactions and technique.

The art of stride analysis is really the ultimate in the intellectual approach to jumping courses, be it hunter or jumper. Knowing beforehand whether the number of strides between two fences is long, medium, or short will make the difference between a planned winning performance or a "lucky" good round. The rider, either by walking the course beforehand or by watching several other horses go over the course, is able to take note of the number of strides between fences of relative proximity and, what's more important, the space needed to get that number of strides.

For example, with the average thoroughbred horse of 16.1 hands, a normal hand-gallop pace is needed to jump an in-and-out twenty-four feet apart in one stride or a thirty-six-foot combination in two strides. With the same horse, the pace must be slowed down to jump a twenty-one-foot in-and-out or a thirty-three-foot one in the same number of strides. This stride analysis can be observed and used for fences five, six and seven strides away, although greater distances apart are better left up to the rider's eye alone, as too many variables can take place within this larger range. It is important to note here that the *number* of strides is not as important a factor as the *pace* required for that number of strides. For instance, two jumps might be five strides apart on a hunter course in a ring. It is imperative to know whether one should ride the line at a slow gallop, a normal gallop, or a faster gallop to meet each fence at the ideal spot. Naturally, the closer the fences are to one another, the more important it is for the rider to know his striding. Only as an occasional exercise should the rider count strides to himself (one, two, three—) as this distracts his timing and natural feel. He should concentrate rather on the prearranged pace and his "eye" to look for a distance.

While on the subject of "looking for a distance" or "developing one's eye," let me state that these are terms related to one's timing. Timing of the horse's take-off is absolutely necessary for any performance to be consistent and of a high caliber. The greatest horse in the world is unable to prearrange his take-off at just the right time over every jump in the show ring. This is simply due to the fact that show-ring jumping of any kind is unnatural—the space is limited; the fences vary in color, height, shape, and breadth; and there are turns to contend with, as well as many other unnatural factors. It is only through the intelligence and talent of the rider helping the clever, talented horse negotiate a series of man-made obstacles that a performance up to modern standards may be predicted. A horse that is hindered by too much "hand riding" is at just as much disadvantage as the animal abandoned by the "passenger." Needless to say, it takes the combined efforts of two very talented living beings to win in horse show competition today.

As far as the actual teaching of timing is concerned, *forget it!* In my experience, it is the one thing in riding that must come by itself in a natural, unhurried way. It is an inner feeling, almost a sixth sense, and the more a rider is allowed to listen to his instincts, the better off he'll be. Occasionally, when working on release, I'll coincide it with the correct take-off point and in this way give the rider the feeling of "when it's right." However, I do want the pupil to acquire this intangible something as much as possible on his own.

Often I have sought *indirect* approaches to timing problems. There are several characteristics that always seem to accompany a rider with a poor eye. The first and foremost seems to be a nervous temperament. The more a person worries, the more he anticipates trouble, and this is the archenemy of good timing— the inability to wait quietly until seeing a distance fairly near the fence. One must wait and let the distance happen, it cannot be pushed or hurried. A very popular theory, with which I wholly disagree, is that the farther away from a fence a rider can see his distance, the better a rider is. This to me is wrong, because the farther away from the fence the rider sees his distance, the more room there is left to chance what is called "guessing for the take-off point!" The great riders never seem hurried or eager to find their "spot" but, rather, wait it out and let definite decisions come *to* them.

Hands are very indicative of a rider's temperament, and good hands (steady, relaxed hands) usually correspond with a good eye. Therefore it becomes apparent that the most direct approach to improve upon one's timing is not to worry about the timing itself so much as steadying the whole rider in his approach to the fence, principally by stressing stillness and immobility of his hands. The adage of "Sit still" or "Keep your hands still" is really not far from the truth. Regardless of more modern riding techniques, it *works!!*

One of my favorite exercises to encourage relaxation and an "eye" for distance utilizes three zones approaching a fence. The first zone is coming around a turn at the end of the ring where the rider concentrates on regulating his horse's pace, balance, and bend. The second zone is coming out of the turn; here the rider relaxes on his horse, mostly in the feel of his horse's mouth, and waits to see the distance to the jump. The third zone occurs from the moment there is a distance until the take-off point. During this zone the rider, for the most part, simply balances his horse by sinking down into his crotch.

## EQUITATION PERFORMANCES

The finished show-ring equitation performance requires four factors: style, performance, consistency, and theatricality. If any one of these vital ingredients is lacking, there is little chance of victory when competing at the top. Naturally each rider has his stronger points, but the aim should be perfection in each one of these categories.

Style simply means the position of the rider's body during all of his equestrian work, be it on the flat or over fences. A rider's style at an advanced level should be classic, yet his own; and it should be, by now, completely automatic. There should be rare instances indeed when style need be sacrificed for function. It is virtually impossible for a rider to be in any contention at all in top equitation competition without his own stamp of a classic position. The most memorable impression a judge can have is the "picture" of a rider on his horse. Unfortunately, style goes hand in hand with the rider's conformation—"riding build." Nonetheless, some of the most classic-looking riders have had to overcome some of their own personal physical problems. It is my contention that every rider should refine his position to the best of his potentialities.

When discussing performance in equitation the horse *must* be taken into account. Not only must the rider be able to ride and function, but his horse also must be physically and mentally up to the job. It is, naturally, best to fit the horse's build to the rider's build. In other words, a short-legged girl should be mounted on a 15.3-hand, narrow lightweight, not a 16.3-hand, big-barreled middleweight. Conformation adjustment must be taken into account for the "picture" to look right.

An equitation horse must also be talented and tractable. He must move with comfortable, smooth gaits and have enough animation to "carry" the rider forward, moving neither tensely nor sluggishly. A horse with too hot a temperament will often blow up at just the crucial time, whereas a dull plodder never allows the rider to be subtle and polished—he always has to *ride* this kind! Especially nowadays, when so many equitation classes are held over modified jumper courses, the jumping ability of the horsemanship horse is more important than ever. He must be able to jump a three-foot nine-inch course easily and be able quickly and cleverly to adjust his strides for the trappy distances. He must turn well and be boldly adaptable to new environments and conditions. In other words, a spooky, suspicious horse is hardly suited to the almost "gimmicky" conditions of present-day equitation. To sum up, a good equitation horse should be reasonably attractive, athletic, sensible, obedient, and willing to co-operate with his rider's many different demands.

Consistency is a joint effort of both horse and rider. Both must be talented enough to repeat over and over again the requirements that must be met without mistakes. A consistent combination is one that judges learn to count on and look for and *expect* to pin. This kind of combination is very important to a judge, especially when the rounds have been poor and he has seen nothing really worthy of a ribbon. Consistency must include precision during flat tests and also over a variety of courses. No rider can possibly be precise without having developed a good eye; and so, along with style and performance, a top equitation rider must be consistent.

## SHOWMANSHIP

The art of showmanship, or theatricality, is really the frosting on the cake. It just tops off all the other good points already mentioned. Some people have an inborn sense of theatricality which, I suppose, is directly associated with the ego. They are able to project outwardly a feeling of superiority and competence and, without being terribly obvious, take advantage of every opportunity to be seen at their best. This quality can best be noticed in groups on the flat. For instance, in warming up for an open equitation class on the flat, the sharp rider works his horse in shoulder-in, counter canter, extensions, and collection, rather than just trotting around the ring. This attracts the judge to a rider who knows and is able to do something. In large classes, the rider with showmanship presents himself and his horse to the judge in a good light at every opportunity—he is seen and not hidden by the mob! On the other hand, if something should go wrong, he is the first to stay out of sight. A wise

106. *Strength through knowledge.* Katie Monahan's success story is written all over her face in this picture. She knows exactly what she wants to do on a horse, and through her complete technical control she is able to do it. PHOTO BY BUDD

107. *Effortless power*. Katie Monahan and "the Jones Boy" show how easy it is to jump a mountainous square oxer when the basics are there—namely talent, education, and hard work. PHOTO BY BUDD

108. *Picture-book form*. Fred Bauer, whom I taught in his early years and Ronnie Mutch taught later, is a real demonstration of a good rider who also rides by the book. His conformation, angles, and basic form have produced this near-perfect equitation shot. PHOTO BY BUDD

109. *Workmanlike polish*. James Hulick, from his tailored clothes to his horse's condition to his excellent form, is a study in show ring presentation; yet there are no artificial frills. He and "Tiny's Thoughts" are the epitome of an equitation-junior hunter combination.

110. *Riding a junior jumper with form*. Anna Jane White, one of the demonstrators pictured earlier in this book, shows an aggressive attitude and a powerful lower leg. The junior jumper can and should be ridden correctly and with style.
PHOTO BY BUDD

111. *A positive ride.* Anna Jane White is shown here giving her well-known "Rivet" a strong, driving ride over a spooky jump. Her toes are out a bit, and her back a bit round, both indicative of a positive ride. (R. D. Mutch, trainer)

112. *Class will tell*. The only thing that overshadows the enormity of Leslie Burr's talent is her extraordinary appeal on a horse. She not only gives every horse a wonderfully positive, free ride, but she also decorates a horse better than any hunter rider in America today. PHOTO BY BUDD

113. *Relaxed concentration*. Buddy Brown and his legendary "Sandsablaze" are showing us all how easily it can be done with the proper mental attitude. Both are doing their job perfectly, yet without a trace of stiffness. PHOTO BY BUDD

114. *Graduating to Grand Prix*. Though Buddy Brown's head is down a bit, notice how similar horse and rider are to the preceding photo, both in attitude and technique. Basics stand fast no matter how large the fence. PHOTO BY BUDD

115. *Freedom.* Buddy Brown is giving "Sandsablaze" a long crest release; the reins are slack, and the horse is totally free to use his head and neck. This is the ultimate in reward over a wide oxer.

116. *Strong yet smooth.* A businesslike approach, a calm attitude, smooth and invisible aids, consistency, beautiful form—all of these ingredients make for a winning ride. Katherine Burdsall and "Old Salt" usually win! PHOTO BY BUDD

117. *Elegance on horseback.* Cynthia Hankins is nothing short of breathtaking when she enters a ring. Her conformation and presence make her almost unbeatable in the equitation division when she produces the round. PHOTO BY BUDD

118. *Will to win*. Eagerness to compete and to win is a beautiful trait. The expressions here of both Colette Lozins and her consistent "Sanman" give that away. Their "go-for-broke" attitude is hard to beat. PHOTO BY BUDD

119. *A beautiful girl on a beautiful horse*. Beauty is as beauty does; and believe me, Francie Steinwedel and "Hot Soup" are able to do! Her awesome appeal and classic technique are irresistible. PHOTO BY FREUDY

120. A *striking combination*. Being big-barreled, "Excitress" can absorb Elizabeth Sheehan's lovely, long leg. Not only do their conformations complement
each other, but their temperaments as well. Both are strong and bold. As an
aside, I do not care for colored braiding yarn. PHOTO BY BUDD

121. *Relaxed precision.* Hugh Mutch is a cool competitor; and he has a relaxed consistency that is truly formidable in any competition. I especially like Hugh's relaxed but flat back. PHOTO BY BUDD

122. *A poet's license.* When one does as much right as Conrad Homfeld (shown here aboard "Balbuco"), one can justify a minor form fault. Conrad is poetry in motion on a horse; and here he is catching up with his horse over a rather wide liverpool by pivoting on his knee. PHOTO BY BUDD

123. *Love for the animal*. Michael Sasso gets the most out of his horse "Dillon" because he sincerely loves the animal. This intangible quality, love, seems to be what separates the "greats" from the "not so greats" in this mystical horse business. To be humane is the greatest gift a horseman can possess!

124. *An Olympian.* This book has been written in the hope that it will help everyone just a little bit in his or her own personal "olympic" quest—be it hacking, hunting, or showing. Michael Matz (shown here aboard "Mighty Ruler") is an Olympian in every sense of the word—as a rider, as a horseman, and especially as a person. PHOTO BY BUDD

125. *A master craftsman*. Bernie Traurig advocates total control over a horse—and gets it. Notice his masterful hands and supple contact with "the Cardinal's" mouth over this large oxer. His hands are unique. PHOTO BY BUDD

126. *Riding against the clock*. Armand Leone and his "Sombre" are a terrifically competitive pair when going for time. Don't worry if a few things slip when riding fast; they will! Here Armand is shown making a sharp right turn in the air. And meaning it! PHOTO BY BUDD

127. *Stay off your horse's back*. Dennis Murphy and his indefatigable "Tusca-loosa" are giving their all to clear this mammoth oxer. Dennis is not only en-couraging his horse, but what is more important, he is not hindering him. Another sometimes necessary instance of sacrificing a bit of form to help one's horse. PHOTO BY BUDD

128. *The fairer sex*. It isn't so fair to the boys, though, if the girls ride like Melanie Smith, as she is proving here with her leading-rider sash. What is pleasing me most, though, are the basics. Melanie and "Val de Loire" are both in superb form as they ride and win in a Grand Prix jump-off against the clock; surely a suitable photograph to end the illustrations in this book! PHOTO BY BUDD

show-ring rider has three eyes open, one on his own perform-ance, one on his fellow competitors, and one on the judge.

The turnout of both horse and rider is part of the theatricality. A clean, neat, well-groomed combination is always an eye-catching start. A good braid job in relation to the horse's con-formation is important. By that I mean the number of braids ac-cording to the length of the horse's neck—a long, swan-necked horse should have fewer braids and a short, thick-necked horse should have more braids. Well-tailored, conservative, and cor-rect attire for hunter seat equitation is a *must*. Be sure to stay away from gaudy, bright colors or loud combinations. Gloves al-ways add a dash of distinction and a girl's hair should be done neatly (and kept out of the face at all times!). If crops are carried, they should preferably be of dark brown leather and without any loops attached. A short feathered bat (riding crop) is nice and also discreet. All in all, the complete turnout should be elegant yet conservative and, above all, with taste. What a head start these riders have upon entering the ring!

## HUNTER PERFORMANCES OVER AN OUTSIDE COURSE

Hunter riding over an outside course or a hunter trial course has its special demands and difficulties for the equitation rider who almost always also shows hunters. The great difference between this kind of work and ring work has to do with pace. The ring pace of a hunter compared to that of an outside course is per-haps two or three miles per hour slower, and this, in itself, is rather an adjustment.

In approaching an outside course, I've found it best to begin with trotting work alongside the fences following the track of the course. Circling around the fences or stopping alongside them usually will settle down a high-feeling horse or a rusher. Of course this won't be necessary if the animal is obedient and sta-

ble. After the trotting work has been done, the same procedure
may be done at the canter, again circling or stopping when and
if necessary.

Now is the time to get the feeling for pace. The horse is
sufficiently worked and relaxed and the rider is able to allow him
to increase his speed to a definite hand gallop. It is most important to feel this pace and for the horse and rider to find the
faster rhythm accompanying it before approaching any fences.
As soon as the horse has had a good breather on a loose rein,
schooling should commence.

As in any work over a complete course, we'll divide an outside
course up into segments. The first will be preparation which is
exactly the same as described in the preceding section, according
to the horse's disposition. The circle on approaching the first
fence is also about the same except larger. This will enable the
rider to have more time to pick up his faster pace gradually. As
soon as the pace has been established, the rider concentrates on
riding his first line, probably comprised of three or four fences.
Whereupon he smoothly pulls up. This sequence is then repeated over the remaining parts of the course until the whole
course has been jumped in this piecemeal fashion. Only now,
providing the work so far has been controlled and steady, should
the entire course be attempted. Lines and pace, let me repeat,
should be uppermost in the rider's mind.

The only position requirements that must be adhered to in
riding a hunter are low hands and a light, forward seat. The
hands, regardless of the head carriage of the horse, must work
down by the withers and stay there. This conceals and minimizes any mouth or head problems and psychologically gives the
impression of an easy horse to ride. The light, forward position
also enhances the picture by adding fluidity and grace, and the
rider in this seat does not distract from the horse by adding excess motion. In short, a hunter performance should be presented
to the judges in such a way that the rider decorates the horse
and adds to the effortless look of the whole. He in no way

should become obvious and apparent. A hunter is an agreeable mount to ride to hounds and should be, at all costs, made to look agreeable whether he is or not!

## JUMPER PERFORMANCES

This book is certainly not intended to explore the more advanced training of the open jumper rider but, rather, to substantiate all the necessary work leading up to that level. Riders with a solid background of equitation and hunter riding most definitely have the foundation needed to begin making the transition into riding bigger courses, with tighter turns and the added dimension of speed, and they especially have some of the preparatory exercises (gymnastics) given open jumpers.

Three of the most basic exercises commonly in use to develop the horse's maximum physical potential and mental stability include: the cavalletti (rails on the ground to trot over), the no-stride in-and-out, and the tight one- and two-stride combination. There is an endless variety of combining these three basic gymnastics and, of course, it is then necessary to incorporate the long-distance combinations too. Also there are a variety of exercises on circles and turns used to introduce horse and rider to "time" riding. As I've said, the work at this level is a step beyond the hunter seat equitation level. It requires infinite imagination and technical variety, and to cover jumper schooling and showing will really need another book. Meanwhile, for those of you who are ready to start simple jumper riding, I will mention two very important position variations from that of hunter riding. In exact contrast to the low hand and light forward seat used to complement the long forward balance of the galloping hunter, the jumper rider should raise his hands a bit, sit up straighter and deepen his seat. This change of the rider's balance to the vertical and the raising of the horse's head and neck tend to shift the horse's weight from front to rear which is exactly what we want. The lighter the horse is on his forehand and the more he is crouched on his hocks, the freer and more athletic his forehand will become. Absolute obedience, sufficient impulsion (at all times), and balance (lightness of the forehand) are three main keys to this task at hand; and the rider must adjust himself to the most favorable position to regulate and maintain these necessary prerequisites.

FACTORS OF THE JUMP

Before finishing this section on advanced work over fences, I'd like to mention five indispensable factors that are present during every jump that is ever jumped. While these ingredients may range from being so poorly presented that they seem unrecognizable, to being so beautifully executed that they appear effortless, nonetheless each one of them is always there.

The first factor must be considered the track of the jump, be it a straight, perpendicular line to the center of the fence, a diagonal line (angle jumping), or a curving line (jumping while turning). There is always a track, whether good or bad.

The second factor has to do with speed. And really, when talking about speed we're talking about pace and stride; it's all the same thing. As the speed is slowed, the stride shortens, and as the pace picks up, the stride lengthens. Every jump is approached at a certain speed, sometimes determined by the rider, sometimes by the problem of the jump or series of jumps, or, alas, sometimes by the horse!

The next factor, and this is not the same thing as speed, is impulsion. Each different type of jump requires a different amount of impulsion from each individual horse. Impulsion is animation and energy. Naturally, when the speed picks up so does the impulsion, and when we slow down the impulsion follows suit.

Often, a problem calls for a slow pace and short stride yet great impulsion. And this, as a rule, is up to the rider to maintain. Now, of course there are lots of hot horses that maintain their own abundance of impulse no matter how slow they are going. These same horses, though, have too much impulsion going for them when working with speed. It is really only through experience that one develops a sixth sense and always has enough RPMs for the specific job at hand. Your great open jumper riders know this for a fact.

Now we come to balance on the approach to an obstacle, our fourth factor. Balance, as we've said, is lightness of forehand. Or to put it another way, making sure that the horse's weight is sufficiently taken off his shoulders and put to his hocks. Balance can be accomplished in three ways: one, by raising his head; two, by engaging his hocks; or three, by doing those two together. Lateral balance is also important. That is balance from side to side, rather than from front to back. The rider's sense of balancing his horse is vitally important. It may take years to develop this sense through experience, while some, just as with impulsion, have a natural instinct for it.

Our fifth factor, distance, is the one most talked about and worried over by all horsemen. We are talking about the comfortable take-off zone to the jump. Naturally, this, too, varies with each horse at each jump and takes years and years for the average rider to gauge accurately. It is also known as timing, or "eye" for a distance, or seeing one's stride. It is the ability to gauge a horse's stride to the base of the obstacle. One should look at the highest element of the obstacle and his feel or sixth sense will tell him where he is. Of course, finding a distance to a fence is inevitably intertwined with our preceding four factors. The five basics are "musts" for every fence. If one or several of them are off kilter, it is impossible to negotiate a good jump.

PART FOUR

# Going to
# Horse Shows

# Horse Shows —
# Just a Test

At the outset of this part I'd like the reader to compare a horse show with an examination in school. Both are indicative of the thoroughness of one's homework and present degree of one's skill and, as far as I'm concerned, of nothing more or less. Once the success of the test outweighs learning the subject, the whole point is lost. Ribbons at horse shows are simply a tangible reward for all the hard work and riding preparation. While I wouldn't expect to undertake an exam until sufficiently ready at least to pass, I would not send in my entry blank for a horse show nor write out a check until my horse and I were ready to put in a creditable performance. If you are a layman and do not have a teacher to give you the word as to whether or not you are up to going to a horse show, I recommend that you seek an honest professional opinion. An experienced eye who's been around will know for sure how you'd stack up to the competition and whether or not you were up to the class requirements.

A very good procedure that even the most experienced follow is to go to a horse show with a green horse and just ride around the grounds during the day. If it's a small show, post (late) entries may be accepted and classes entered at random. This system also works with green riders, as it introduces showing to

them in a casual way. As a rule, it's best in the very beginning
with both novice horse and rider to stick to flat classes and not
get involved with jumping quite yet. It's harder to get into real
trouble on the flat, and just being at the horse show should give
you a basis of comparison. By using common sense and seeking
professional advice, the new exhibitor should get off to a good
start; the overambitious usually fall on their faces, and the super-
timid never get off the ground. The American Horse Shows
Association (AHSA) has very soundly provided its horse shows
with equitation classes of different degrees of difficulty and of
limitations for riders according to their winnings in past horse
shows. This keeps contestants on a relatively even par as to age
and ability and is also a very sound way of encouraging riders to
stay in their bracket (such as a maiden rider, one who has never
won a blue ribbon at a recognized horse show or a novice, one
who hasn't won three blue ribbons). There are also limit and
intermediate equitation classes and classes for those under a certain age such as ten, twelve, or fourteen. So when one is starting
out in the equitation division, one can more or less let the results
be the guide as to how fast to progress into more difficult competition. I rarely, if ever, allow any of my students under twelve to
enter a Maclay, AHSA Medal, or U. S. Equestrian Team
(USET) class. Nor do those riders who have not won six blue
ribbons over jumps and who are ineligible for the limit class go
into those more difficult events. Let a rider prove himself
through ability and experience. This is a foolproof way of not
overfacing and pushing a youngster, which I consider very important. While the riding needn't be terribly sophisticated at
these minor levels, basic position and control are being judged
and must be there rather accurately. It would be wise, in any
event, before getting too involved with horse shows to become
familiar with the American Horse Shows Association and its excellent Rule Book. This would considerably clarify an area in
which there's a lot of confusion to the newcomer. But now let's
get on with the subject at hand and see what's involved in being
a horse show exhibitor.

# 9
# Presenting the Horse

## THE CORRECT MOUNT

Very rarely, with competition as keen as it is today, does the school horse have the quality or the talent to present an equitation rider to his best advantage. As a rule, the most useful school horses, as far as temperament is concerned, are Half-Breds, while nine out of ten of today's show horses are thoroughbreds. I remember when I started showing in horsemanship classes that one could easily get away with showing a good jumping school horse. Not so today. There are simply too many beautiful horse-rider combinations showing now, so it is a distinct disadvantage to ride a "clunker." Keep the school horses at home for lesson and drill work and go out and select something with a bit of quality for the show ring.

For most junior exhibitors, going to horse shows is too expensive to have a horse that is just an equitation mount. That is why I insist on my junior horses being potentially able to compete in some other junor division. If a rider qualifies early in the year for the Maclay and Medal finals and can only compete in the open and the USET classes, he's really "up the creek" with nothing left to ride in at the horse shows. However, if his horse is at least adequate in the junior hunter or jumper division, he'll be able to keep busy, keep practicing, and keep riding throughout the show season. This is most important as there is nothing more tentative than a rider who has had too little ring work come finals time. I, for one, have found that the finals are most likely to be won by riders who have had constant ring exposure all year long. That is why I suggest selecting a horse with more than one string to his bow if possible. Of course, there is the exceptional horse who, for some reason or other such as way of moving or perhaps soundness, cannot possibly win as a hunter and doesn't have the scope to perform as a junior jumper, yet is a fabulous equitation horse. This horse should not be left at home but should be used at the show for perhaps several different riders.

In selecting the correct mount, the first and foremost consideration is fitting the horse to the rider, the two most important aspects being the mental temperament of both and their physical conformations. In co-ordinating personalities one must remember that there are two kinds of riders: overriders and underriders. In general it's best to suit the aggressive, active, overrider, one who demands horses to react, to a horse of either a sluggish or "bully" (independent) nature. This kind of horse needs an authoritative, strong ride and will allow that sort of rider to look his best. On the other hand, the passive, quiet underrider will shine on a quick, sensitive, often "hot" type of horse. This kind of rider is reluctant to tell or demand his mount much of anything and that is just the right way to get the best performance out of this kind of animal. Of course, another aspect of a rider's personality that must be analyzed most carefully by the instructor before any selection can be made is his degree of mental and/or physical fear, mental fear being the fear of making a mistake and physical fear being that of getting hurt. Either of these fears can and usually do tend to make people override or underride. Needless to say, the more a rider's nerves are affected by riding horses either at home or at a show, the more seasoned and reliable his horse should be. "Green prospects" are not in the cards at this time for people with an excess of fear in any direction.

Now let's get on to fitting horse and rider together vis-à-vis conformation. Basically there are two extremes of body types, short and long. It's easy to say that the short-legged "shrimp" should have a small horse and the long, leggy "drink of water" should be mounted on a big horse. This, unfortunately, does not always hold true and is not an accurate enough guide. Most important in this department is the horse's barrel, either one to take up a good deal of leg or one to permit very little leg not to have much to get around. I prefer the short-bodied, long-legged person to have a smallish, big-barreled horse and the tall, leggy one to have a tall animal also with plenty of middle. A little tiny tot should have a small, narrow horse all the way around (and with most children under ten or eleven years old, ponies are the best), while the stubby-legged, long-trunk rider needs a bigger, taller horse who is rather slab-sided. In general, this should be a fairly good guide in matching a pair, and it's better not to get too much more specific in physical particulars as one must now concentrate on a talented, capable beast, able to do the job.

After the determination has been made that horse and rider "get along well" and "make a pretty picture," the instructor and purchaser must make absolutely sure that this horse has what it takes for the equitation division. There are several key characteristics that simply must be present. First, is the horse sound and attractive? You definitely don't need a strip horse completely without blemishes, but make sure that whatever blemishes he has won't make him serviceably unsound. This a reliable veterinarian must decide on. A really ugly horse, as a rule, won't do. Try to buy a horse that, even if not beautiful, is at least somewhat attractive. Many parents go overboard on looks and this is wrong, especially when it is at the expense of more valuable assets. All I'm saying is to look for some sort of eye appeal, even just a good color. The next step is to check this animal's way of moving. Is he a long enough mover to be able to handle spread jumps and long combinations, yet short enough not to be awkward and clumsy? Are his gaits smooth enough to present an invisible rider or is he choppy and rough? Make sure also that his trot is even; there is nothing worse than a "hitcher" making a strong trot in a USET class. Another fault which may or may not be correctable is a "cross-canterer." This can be an annoying and difficult habit to deal with. Again, don't get me wrong; your horse does not have to be a top hunter under saddle, he just can't have any serious drawbacks in his way of going.

Manners are the next consideration. The more I work with equitation horses, the more manners count. There is nothing more painful than to put a lot of time into a horse that is too keen, sour, a deadhead, erratic, or in possession of a chronic vice such as bucking, rearing, or shying. Look for a horse that is co-operative, a keen but submissive sort of ride. Remember that many of the temperament faults that you see when he is being shown for sale are more often than not a real part of that horse. An equitation horse must want to learn. He must also be patient.

Jumping talent is an entity unto itself and to me probably the most significant single factor in selecting a horse for the hunter seat equitation division. All that we've mentioned before goes down the drain if there aren't eight good fences. Most people dislike "stoppers" as much as anything, and so do I. Usually horses that are habitual stoppers have some kind of mechanical trouble getting up and over a fence, a symptom rather than a disease. There are enough horses that really don't mind jumping at all for you to waste time with the others. Once the fact has been established that this horse is a willing jumper and not the reverse, pay attention to his legs. If he folds in front and is fairly conventional behind, you're all right. Beware of the knee-hanger. Never, never buy a horse that dangles his legs, since at best he's not good enough and at worst dangerous. It's very rare indeed that this physical fault is corrected. In fact, he must be able to jump comfortably a three-foot nine-inch fence with about a four-foot spread. This will insure him being a good

USET horse with room to spare for the Medal and Maclay. Just what is needed in today's show ring.

All in all, a good equitation mount should be agreeable looking. He should be pliable, mannerly, and free moving both over fences and on the flat. Athletic ability and handiness over fences are a must if he is to jump smoothly over moderately difficult combinations and off tight turns. This kind of horse very often is a "jack-of-all-trades" as far as other divisions are concerned, even though he's master of none except the horsemanship route. Often horses that just don't quite have it in the big hunter-jumper leagues fit the bill to perfection. Once the right package of horse and rider have been put together, all that is needed is show-ring mileage and proper training.

## A PROPERLY TURNED OUT HORSE

After all is said and done, a horse in the peak of condition, groomed to perfection, and with all the little finishing touches put to an animal for the show ring has got to be miles ahead of his ragged competition as soon as he enters the ring. This can mean the difference between several ribbon placements or even, when competition is keen, being out of the ribbons completely and winning a class. I can't emphasize the general appearance of the horse's condition enough. Not only does it insure that a horse is more fit to perform his job as well as possible, but it is also the very first step in psychologically impressing the judge. And that's what showing is all about, to prove to the judge in every way possible that you are tops in your class.

To get a horse conditioned both internally and externally for the show ring cannot be done in a few days; it literally takes months. The proper balance between a good feeling program and an adequate working schedule is the foundation for this conditioning. Needless to say, daily, thorough grooming, turning the horse out in the pasture for relaxation, attention to the horse's teeth, worming, shoeing, etc., all contribute toward putting the package together. The end result must be a fairly fit horse in good weight (not too fat or too thin) whose coat is glossy and healthy in appearance. Of course, each horse has different requirements in feeding and working. Some horses must be fitter than others, too, and this usually corresponds directly to temperament.

During actual performance of the horse in his classes, there is nothing so important as his mouth and his way of moving. Both of these aspects can be controlled and improved to a degree through proper care of teeth and correct shoeing. I have all my horses' teeth "floated" once a year. This means that all the rough edges of the horse's teeth are filed and smoothed down. As far as shoeing is concerned, again each horse is different. Hunters should move as closely to the ground as possible. Therefore I often prefer a light plate rather than a shoe of a heavier weight. Jumpers can have a little more shoe, and I feel that calks, either temporary or permanent, give a little more grab in going for time or on slick turf. This, again, changes according to the individual. These are the little particulars, though, that do spell the difference between winning and losing; and when great time and money are being spent, nothing should be overlooked.

Once the horse has been brought into "show shape" over a period of time and is "looking good," we are ready to spruce him up a day or two before shipping out. Trimming and mane-pulling are now in order. A show horse's mane should just be long enough to be able to put up a nice neat short braid job. If the mane is too long, the braids will be too big and not very attractive; but if too short, it will be hard to braid at all. Don't, under any circumstances, cut a mane. The work should be done completely by pulling out the underneath hairs with a mane comb. As far as the horse's tail is concerned, the more it's left alone the better. Some people prefer to bang a tail halfway below the hock. If this is done evenly with a scissors it looks fine and is simply a matter of individual preference.

Trimming with the ear clippers comes next and should include all long hairs around the muzzle, jaw, throat, eyes, ears, poll, fetlocks, and coronary band. A meticulous trimming job takes very little time and should be attended to every couple of weeks while the horse is on the road showing. It just polishes and tidies up the picture. Of course, if the horse needs a complete clipping, this should be done about a week ahead of the horse show so the poor beast doesn't look like a skinned rabbit. Clipping is an art unto itself and should be done by an experienced hand or under a guiding eye. "Amateur night" can be spotted in a minute by a bad clipping job and this really is inexcusable in presenting a horse to the judge.

Preparing a horse to go into the ring is a detailed task often done before sun-up. Usually the first thing gotten out of the way is braiding of the horse's mane and, more often than not, his tail. As a rule, short-necked horses require more braids to give them length of front while long-necked horses need fewer braids. Twelve to fifteen braids should be minimum, though, for any horse. Many people braid with yarn which can be done well, although I prefer braiding by sewing in. Never, never braid with elastic bands for the show ring. Use them at home to train a mane to stay over on one side of the neck. Manes are not difficult for anyone to learn how to do and tails become easier and look better the more one practices. I would advise the newcomer to take time at home and really learn how to braid well before going to the show.

Cleanliness of horse and tack are next in line to check before that first class. Gray horses, although they are real eye-catchers in groups, are quite a nuisance to keep clean and they usually require a shampoo bath a day or two before the show. This also applies to any horse with white legs. Once the horse is basically clean, all we need do is give him a good grooming in the morning. While tack should be kept scrupulously clean at all times for the comfort of the horse and the good of the leather, just before show time an extra check should be made, with strict attention to any metal parts, which should be well polished.

Now that the horse is braided, groomed, and his tack spotless, he's ready to be schooled and shown. Just before entering the ring, either to perform or jog for soundness, he can be gone over with a rub rag and his feet painted with hoof dressing. Just remember that the total picture is being judged and the horse's turnout is the first impression. For more specific details of horse care and stable management, I suggest you consult any of the good books on the subject such as M. A. Stoneridge's *A Horse of Your Own*, published by Doubleday, or any of the official U. S. Pony Club manuals.

## TACK

Apart from insisting on cleanliness, I want to add a few words about tack and its adjustment. Though I'm really not interested in getting involved in a dispute over types of bits or makes of saddles, there are a couple of things pertaining to tack that are important.

As everybody knows, different bits cause different reactions with horses' mouths. I, myself, believe in the snaffle—any variety of snaffle depending on the horse's mouth problem, from a thick egg-butt snaffle to a double twisted-wire one. I like the snaffle for several reasons, one being that it's the simplest, most "uncluttered" bit to put in a horse's mouth; another is that the jointed action of the snaffle is against the corners of the mouth when a horse pulls. Also, riders of intelligence must quickly realize that the bit is just a part of control. Leg, seat, voice, and the hands along with the bit direct the horse. That is why good riders, riders who are technically sound and strong, are able to ride al-

most anything with just a plain snaffle. However, do not overlook the Pelham; some horses simply go well in a Pelham and
that's a matter of fact. A double bridle, though, seems as a rule
to be too much in a horse's mouth, and I myself don't like kimberwickes at all.

A major problem I've noticed with many people is that they
don't know how to adjust bits. A rule of thumb that is quite accurate, in regard to the height of the bit in the horse's mouth, is
to have two or three wrinkles show in the corners with a jointed
snaffle and one slight wrinkle with a Pelham or any other
straight-bar bit. Make sure that the bit is a comfortable width in
the horse's mouth, not too wide or too narrow. Often a bit
hangs too low in a horse's mouth and tongue problems then
develop.

A popular bridle accessory that I feel is overindulged in is the
dropped noseband. Unless a horse opens his mouth upon the
slightest action of the bit, I don't believe it is that necessary. In
other words, use it if there is particular difficulty in the "mouth-
opening department"; otherwise, a regular cavesson will do the
job just as well.

As far as a saddle is concerned, it's strictly a matter of taste as
to the make. As long as it fits the rider and the horse comfortably, the pommel doesn't rest on the withers (in which case a
pad should be used), and the deepest point is in the middle of
the saddle and not back toward the cantle somewhere, everything should be all right. Many people swear by one make or another, but that is strictly a matter of preference.

Martingales have always been a subject of great dispute.
Again, I believe that the choice of martingale, be it running or
standing, should be left up to the individual's preference. By
limiting a horseman as to his equipment (providing it's humane), a situation that has arisen through certain show jumping
associations' rulings, training beliefs and artistic independence
are severely stifled. In relation to the levels of riding discussed in

this book, I feel that the standing martingale is very beneficial in work over fences with most horses, and I have several strong arguments in favor of it.

The standing martingale doesn't have to hold a horse's head down. It simply limits the degree to which a horse can escape the action of the bit by raising or throwing his head up. This limiting action of the martingale acts as a safety device in two ways. First, it almost eliminates the chance of a rider getting hit in the face as he's jumping a course. And, secondly, the horse is able to escape the action of the hand just so far by raising his head, thereby being more controllable, especially for the less advanced rider. Both of these factors, I've found, not only provide safety but also a more permanent "frame of horse," which is a definite asset for a jumping performance. Without any martingale, the average horse will often escape the action of the hand at just the crucial time, while a standing martingale is always there as a stopgap.

The principal difference between the standing and running martingales really relates to where they physically affect the horse. The standing martingale, attached to the cavesson, exerts pressure on the upper hard bones of the nose, while the running martingale, through the action of the reins and the bit, hits the sensitive bars of the mouth. The paradox to me, of course, has always been that when a horse is punished on the bars of the mouth his defense is always to throw his head forward and up. And it is a familiar sight to see a horse "running his head" in this manner, trying (successfully) to evade the martingale and the hand! I feel that mouth problems are encouraged and control is lost at fast paces to a great extent without the standing martingale. This is a matter of individual preference; and each school of thought is strongly committed, convinced that one way or the other way is right!

The two auxiliary reins most commonly in use, reins that artificially help the rider fix the horse's head into a flexed position, are the side reins and draw reins. Personally I'm against riding horses in either, as I feel they are a crutch and give the rider a false sense of accomplishment. Rather than putting the horse to the bit with the correct use of hands and legs, he is holding his horse into an apparently correct position by use of force. These rein aids do not teach a rider to feel how to ride; they actually slow down the process and mitigate his desire to experiment through using his own natural aids. Now there are, of course, exceptional circumstances where time is of the essence and short cuts may be necessary in order to show or sell a horse. These occasions should be rare and evaluated in their true light so no one is deluded into thinking that a real and permanent control is taking place. As a rule I've found that controls exerted through use of these artificial rein aids last as long as the crutch is actually in use and not much longer.

As far as longeing is concerned, that is a different matter. Longeing is a preparation for the horse before being ridden, no more no less. It is certainly no replacement for a horse being ridden properly with a rider on his back. To train the horse from the ground, the rider must replace all of his natural aids with artificial aids—the longe line being his hand, the whip his leg, and, in this case, the side reins acting as rein effects. Without side reins' imposing some kind of disciplined framework during work on the longe line, there is little or no training at all connected with this form of exercise.

All in all, every piece of tack of conventional nature has its time and place in training and showing the horse to his best advantage. No equipment related to horses is more controversial than what the horse wears; and this will most certainly be the case as long as horsemen retain their individuality and imagination in trying to beat out their fellow competitors. Experiment with different tack and equipment. It's both interesting and fun. However, in the long run you'll probably discover that the rider's ability and control over his aids greatly outweighs a "bag of bits!"

# 10

# *What the Rider Should Know*

## A PROPERLY TURNED OUT RIDER

Every rider possesses, to his advantage or disadvantage, whichever the case, a figure for riding. I believe in making the best of what's available and that's that. Really, it's incredible to see what some people can do in spite of not being "built to ride." There are really no exercises off horses that are particularly advantageous to riders save the one of standing on the balls of the feet on a step and pushing down the heels. This does seem to stretch those back tendons and improve a rider's heel flexion when mounted. Another one I recommend to about a third of my riders is to push away from the dinner table. A fat rider is definitely behind the eight ball! Rarely can someone be too thin for this sport unless he be emaciated and weak, which isn't often the case.

In the equitation division, a total picture is being judged and to pretend that a rider's build has no effect on a judge's decision is ludicrous. However, as long as a rider isn't terribly overweight, he usually can compensate for his build by being an extra good "jockey." Someone with limited talent and poor conformation can't hope to win much in this division but should look rather at his participation from the point of view of good experience and education. The training and showing of hunter seat equitation is the greatest background a young horseman can have, insuring a solid riding foundation that will hold him in good stead for the rest of his life. I encourage young riders (up to fifteen or sixteen years old) to go into horsemanship classes for this very reason. I have, however, on rare occasions, suggested to those in their latter teen-age years to concentrate on riding in other divisions. These people usually do not like equitation because of a disadvantage in their conformation or their horse, and it is simply too demoralizing for them to continue at such great odds. Often their riding interest can only be salvaged by showing in other directions.

Anybody can be clean and neat and dress well regardless of his financial position. Some points to remember as far as personal appearance is concerned are: short, conventional haircuts for boys and short hair or hairnets for girls (braids are all right for young pony riders, but no "flowing locks," no matter what!); the less jewelry the better and if worn make sure it's in good taste and inconspicuous (the same goes for any make-up!). Dark leather gloves are never wrong, although not a must unless someone has particularly bad hands, in which case they hide a multitude of sins. Black or very dark navy hunt caps are mandatory (I like derbies, but they are a bit outdated). Select chokers for girls and ties for boys that go well with their different riding jackets. Jackets, both for summer and winter, should be attractive yet conventional and, most important of all, fit well; there is nothing more detrimental to a rider's posture than a loose, baggy coat. Rarely use a black coat in equitation as it presents a somewhat stiff, overly formal picture; dark navy is fine. Breeches should be of any tan, gray, or canary material (never white unless the rider is also dressed for an appointments class). These must also be well fitted, or a sloppy presentation will result. As far as boots are concerned, make sure that they are tall enough to give the rider as much length of leg as possible and fit snugly in the calves. I prefer any black or darkish tan boot (a field boot is nice), preferably without tops. Spur rests are optional as long as they don't position the spur too high on the rider's heel. As far as the spur itself is concerned, I like the moderate "Prince-of-Wales" variety over the sharp "hammerhead," or German, spur. It is most important that the spur run parallel and directly under the heel seam of the boot, not pointing up or down. Riding crops if used should be of dark brown or black, inconspicuous as to color and length. Whenever attention is brought to an artificial aid for any reason, riding problems or horse problems immediately are suspected. All in all, a rider entering a show ring should appear elegant in an understated, conventional way. No part of his riding attire should draw attention to itself and under no circumstances should there be any flashiness. Imagination can enter in subtly tailoring clothing to the rider's build and in co-ordinating colors with the horse.

## GENERAL REQUIREMENTS AND CLASS ROUTINES

Catching the judge's eye with an attractively turned-out horse-rider combination is by no means the whole thing. A good basic position and control over the horse must be apparent upon entering the ring, either on the flat or over jumps. I've found that the position of different parts of the rider's body and the aides for controls advocated in this book are as generally accepted by the American Horse Shows Association judges' roster as any other system, and usually more so. Of course, each judge has been brought up with a specific riding background of his own and this will color his opinion as he closely examines riders in the ring. Fortunately my riding background is almost identical to the system used and recommended by the AHSA in describing the equitation hunter seat in their Rule Book, so that there's no conflict whatsoever in what I teach riders for this division.

In my opinion there are three distinct riding systems in this country today, and every American rider is a product of one or a combination of these three systems. The first one I would term the "Old English hunting" way of riding, riding with the legs forward, feet "home" in the stirrups, and the rider most definitely behind the motion of his horse. This style is most limiting and fortunately becoming extinct. The second style is the one derived from the Fort Riley (U. S. Cavalry School) methods; and while this way has its severe exaggerations, which are now outdated, much of it is natural, fluid, and right for modern showing. The third and newest method of riding, introduced to this country within the past fifteen years or so, is that of the German school. While the good points of this school have greatly advanced precision in riding in the United States today (through a much needed and proper use of dressage), there is always the danger in this kind of riding becoming overly stiff and heavy in the use of the aids. I have actually felt, through experimentation, that one can take points from each of these primary approaches and come up with something balanced and good. That is, in a nutshell, what this book is all about and how my theories have come into being.

Once definite controls and an established position have been set at home, the rider is free to concentrate on getting his horse to perform well at a show. It is much too late to worry about form while in a class. Riding well is all that counts, and if faults are spotted, they must be put off as homework for the next week. One has enough to think of in controlling his horse's pace, smooth transitions, riding proper lines and turns, and getting his fences. The very worst thing an instructor can do to a rider before entering the ring is to clutter his mind. It just makes matters worse.

In a flat equitation class the riders perform in a group until individual tests may be asked. Assuming that control and position are there, the rider must now keep three eyes open—one on himself, one on the other horses in the class, and one on the judge.

First, his own performance at the walk, trot, and canter must be without fault; then he must watch out so others don't upset his horse or cut him off; and lastly (but not least) he must be seen by the judge whenever possible unless his horse is misbehaving. This is what is called "making a pass" and must be done without hindering the other horses or in too obvious a manner. The best way is to find the "holes" in the group and get to them. Circling through the middle of the ring is all right on occasion, but don't do it too often. It becomes a real nuisance to the judge.

Once the call to line up has been made, try to get into the middle of the line, not on an end. In this way you'll not have to be first to do a test if one is asked for. It is better to watch a few others before doing one yourself. Also while standing in line waiting for results, do not lose your position or a feel of your horse. This is a horsemanship class not a hack class! Be sure to remember (this is for the "minority males") to take off your hunt cap whenever you receive a ribbon, no matter what the color!

As far as an equitation class over jumps is concerned, the position and control factors are the same as we've taught in this book. The class routine is rather specific and definite and so we'll go into that now in detail. Obviously the first thing the participant must do is learn the course. He must then concentrate on how to ride this particular course, which involves three major things—lines, turns, and distances between the jumps that are placed close to one another. The lines and turns become fairly obvious almost at once; the "striding" between jumps can be more complex and only by watching several horses with different lengths of stride can the rider determine whether it's a "long two" or a "short three," or on another part of the course whether it's a "nice five" or a "tight five." Stride analysis is becoming more important as the courses become more complex and I'm not going to go into this subject in tremendous detail since that is a subject best left to those studying training of the open jumper. The basic point is that one can figure on the distance from the horse's landing over a jump to the take-off at the next jump and determine the pace needed—slow, medium, or fast—to "meet" the second jump correctly. One should rarely count while riding, as this can be a very artificial crutch; you simply must know ahead of time the pace required from one jump to the next if they are within six strides of one another.

When the rider feels he knows his course and all of its little details as intimately as possible, he's ready to warm up his horse for the class. The amount of time this warm-up takes is determined by the rider and the horse's temperament, the number of classes that particular day, and the severity of the course. A jumping warmup should *always* end on a good note. There is nothing surer than a poor performance following a disastrous preparation. Now the horse should have enough time to catch his breath but not so much time that he gets "cold" before entering the ring.

One's preparatory track includes the ride from the in-gate to the first fence and this usually involves a circle approximately one third of the whole ring in dimension. Any approach smaller than this is hurried and any larger is too time consuming and a bore. There are two ways of riding this preparatory track; one may enter the ring at a posting trot and continue this gait for two thirds of the circle whereupon he takes up his canter from the slow sitting trot and then establishes his pace for the first fence; or he may walk the first third of the circle and then break into a canter and not use the trot work at all. Either method is all right as long as it's planned ahead of time.

In actually riding over the course, the rider should concentrate solely on lines and turns and the pace needed for suitable striding. Smoothness should color all equitation work and any rough spots should be camouflaged as much as possible. One of the great arts in the showing of a horse is to hide what shouldn't be seen and to show off what should. This takes great experience and lots of "cool" and is usually what separates the good ones from the great ones. Once the last fence has been jumped, a gradual, quiet transition should be made back to the walk as horse and rider leave the ring.

This just about covers basic class requirements and routines. Next we'll cover the specialty work for the Maclay, Medal, and USET classes, plus some of the tests set forth by the AHSA for hunter seat riders. While much of this work is for advanced levels only, many novices may find it interesting and helpful to become familiar with the additional demands they may eventually face. There really is no one big step that says to a rider "Now I'm ready for Maclay, Medal, and USET classes." Rather it just happens gradually with time and experience through lots of intermediate steps.

### MACLAY, MEDAL, AND USET CLASSES

While Maclay and Medal classes can be considered the final steps to hunter seat equitation riding, the USET class is more likely the first step and introduction to open jumper riding. All three classes are conducted over intricate jumping courses, while flat work and special tests of an advanced nature are also mandatory. It can't be said often enough that a young rider shouldn't be allowed to enter these classes unless he has thoroughly proved his competence and ability to ride safely in all other classes preceding these, i.e., novice, limit (three to six blue ribbons), age groups, open, and the like. Any short cuts are risky and highly unadvisable and the horses used for these competitions must also be up to the job.

The Maclay class is perhaps the one to try first, as the course will possibly be simpler than the one used in the Medal. It is usually a course of about eight fences, either hunter or jumper type not exceeding three feet six inches. The class is sponsored by the ASPCA and its original idea, to encourage sympathetic horsemen, has certainly worked. Only an educated, intelligent rider can be a kind rider; then it's up to his personality and morals. No matter how charitable an ignorant rider may be, he can't possibly do the best thing for his horse and he is usually cruel without even knowing it. Very rarely do judges judge a Maclay event any differently than any other horsemanship class. A feeling for one's horse, controls that are smooth, and a relaxed position are taken into account. The one main difference inherent in a Maclay class is that a big percentage of those who negotiate the course successfully are also asked to come back and work on the flat. Therefore one's flat work had better match one's proficiency over fences or else one is out of luck. Martingales are allowed on the flat in a class where jumping is part of the whole event and this can be some help to those riders whose horses are difficult to keep down on the bit. Take care not to "goof" if called back to work on the flat as this half of the class counts 50 per cent. I'll be describing in detail later on what flat work may be required in this and other equitation classes. The Maclay finals are held each year at the National Horse Show in Madison Square Garden. It takes a different number of blue ribbons in the different zones around the country to qualify for this event, and it is rather a prestigious happening when one does qualify.

The AHSA Hunter Seat Medal class may or may not arrange a more difficult jumping course than the one for the Maclay. At any rate, it must follow a figure-eight pattern of some sort and two or more of the official tests (discussed in the next section of this chapter) are required of at least the top four contestants. These tests can and do include changing horses, trotting jumps, jumping without stirrups, and often exercises not meant for the novice rider. So again, be ready when attempting the Medal class. Flat work, as a rule, is not used in the Medal as a test. The finals of this particular event are held at some major horse show in the fall of the year. The qualification pattern is similar to that of the Maclay and the prestige of just getting to the finals, let alone getting a ribbon or winning them, is tremendous.

Of the three classes we're now discussing, the USET is definitely the most sophisticated. Almost without exception, I insist upon a rider doing well in Medal and Maclay before allowing him to enter this event. The first phase of this class may be worked on the flat or over fences, depending on the show management. The flat phase includes (besides ordinary walk, trot, and canter) the ordinary sitting trot, strong posting trot, strong canter and counter canter. By the way, remember to stay seated in the saddle for the strong canter; don't assume a galloping stance. In order to show yourself and your horse off to best advantage, try and make sure that the judge gets a good look at what you do best. For example, if your horse performs a strong trot with brilliance and extension, don't hide it on the rail. Or when the order to reverse is called, rather than just turning around, do a turn on the forehand or haunches. It gives the educated, proficient rider that little edge.

Be prepared to ride over a rather demanding course in the jumping phase of a USET class. Not only is this course a bit higher than any other equitation class (up to three feet nine inches) but also various spread jumps, combinations, and changes of direction are usually present. The class came into being to encourage good riding on the open jumper, and the jumper course is what one expects to find. While there is no apparent change in a rider's approach to this class compared to any other equitation class, more proficiency and experience must be present in both the horse and the rider in order to meet the added dimensions and added tests. Let me repeat that this particular competition is not for the limited horse or novice rider and that is why the entry is often smaller than in either Maclay or Medal.

Once the rider has reached the level of being able to compete successfully in these three events, he's really "made" it, so to speak, in the hunter seat equitation division. The greatest fun for me, of course, has been polishing riders at this level, perfecting their controls and course analysis, and cementing a foundation that will enable these young riders to show their horses as hunters and jumpers successfully later on. As far as I've ever been concerned, equitation riding is an end unto itself in that it's the greatest educational step and preparation a rider can take. Only after a rider has left his horsemanship years behind can I consider it just a means to an end. While a child is learning the rudiments of advanced riding and showing, there is no division offered by an official association in the world that is more valuable to equestrian development than this one. About 80 per cent of a rider's technical background can and should be learned while training for and competing in these classes. To go to the top in this particular division is a fine goal and a fantastic achievement, so why not consider it an end unto itself for those who don't go any further? For those who do continue to ride competitively later on, equitation showing can be considered a means to a more extensive goal. Either way, remember that those who've had the advantage and good training of the Hunter Seat Equitation Division are, almost without exception, the ones who win in all phases of adult competition.

### AHSA HUNTER SEAT TESTS

The American Horse Shows Association (AHSA) Hunter Seat Equitation Committee has provided horse show judges with eighteen special tests from which they must choose one or several if they want additional exercises for the contestants in a class. Of course, the degree of difficulty of a particular test determines whether or not it can be used for that particular competition and the tests are listed in the AHSA Rule Book from one to eighteen in order of difficulty. For instance, in a maiden class

(those who have not won a blue ribbon in equitation at a recognized horse show) the judges may use only test number one
—to back up the horse. On the other hand, a novice rider (one
who hasn't yet won three blues) could be required to back up,
gallop and halt, make a figure eight at a trot and/or canter, pull
up and halt between fences, or even jump a figure-eight course.
To go on and complete the picture, a Medal rider must be prepared, in addition to the tests already mentioned, to jump low
fences at a walk and trot as well as at a canter (the maximum
height for a trotting fence is three feet), ride without stirrups
(drop and pick up stirrups), dismount and mount, make a half-
turn on the forehand, execute a serpentine at a trot and/or canter on correct lead demonstrating simple or flying changes of
lead, do a figure eight at canter or correct lead demonstrating
flying changes of lead, change leads down center of ring demonstrating a simple or flying change of lead, change horses or ride
a strange horse supplied by committee, canter on the counter
lead (no more than eight horses may counter canter at one
time), make a half-turn on the haunches, or present a demonstration ride of approximately one minute.

You can see how comprehensive this test list is, yet it fore-
warns contestants as to what they may be asked to do and always keeps the judges from getting carried away by asking the
impossible. In order to make sure that everyone, even the specta-
tors, understands the ride-off, the test must be announced pub-
licly over the loudspeaker beforehand. Let's look back at the list
in detail and see what each one is all about.

*Test 1—Back up.* Any rider up to walking, trotting, and cantering in a horse show also should have been taught how to back
up. Usually this test is asked of the riders after they have lined
up, either individually or as a whole group. One should back a
horse up as follows: Take a feel of your horse's mouth with your
hands correctly placed over and slightly in front of the withers;

close your hands on the reins so as to prevent the horse from moving forward; then tell him to back up by closing your legs and driving him into the bit. During the backing procedure the rider should look straight ahead to insure a straight back up. Don't look down at your horse. Smoothness, promptness, and precision are being judged and often a judge will request that the horse back up a certain number of steps. Remember, in training a horse in this exercise, to strengthen your driving aids, not your hands, to get horses to back. If the closed leg isn't enough to push him back, use a little cluck or stick to accent the leg aid. Once the horse has backed the desired number of steps, ask him to go forward immediately so as not to learn the habit of dropping behind the bit.

*Test 2—Hand gallop and halt.* While maiden riders shouldn't risk working at the gallop, novices most certainly should be introduced to this pace. There are two possibilities of rein aids used to halt a horse from the gallop—the direct rein and the pulley rein—but only use the direct rein in equitation, as some judges feel that the pulley rein is too rough and severe. Almost without exception, the judge will call for the halt at a specific point and it is most important that the rider try to stop exactly at that spot. If the rider has been called out of line to demonstrate galloping and stopping, he should pick up his canter early enough so that he has time to move into the galloping pace and then show his halt. There should be nothing rushed about this test. As he moves off from his canter depart into his hand gallop, the rider assumes his two-point galloping seat and makes sure that his horse holds the pace, which should be between fourteen and sixteen miles per hour. As the halting point is being approached, the hands close on a direct rein aid, the rider's weight shifts to the rear by the opening of his hip angle, and a subtle "Whoa" may be used providing it's not too loud. Needless to say, the halt must commence early enough to stop on time, yet not so early that it is dragged out. This really depends solely on the horse's responsiveness. After stopping, it is best to stand quietly in position for a moment or two.

*Test 3—Figure eight at trot, demonstrating change of diagonals.* A formula for this test, if called for at the short end of the ring, would be as follows: First, the rider finds the middle line of the ring which runs through the figure eight's point of intersection to the focal point; he rides down this imaginary line at a slow sitting trot; just before the point of intersection, he undertakes the posting trot assuming the left diagonal and the figure eight commences with a circle to the right. He recrosses the point of intersection, changing diagonals, and makes a circle to the left. The figure eight is concluded by the rider stopping his horse facing his focal point at the end of the ring. The stop must be smooth, definite, and straight, and it should be exactly at the point of intersection. This procedure creates an accurate execution of this often-used test. Remember that regardless of where in the ring the figure is called for, it is up to the rider to establish a point of intersection by finding a focal point.

*Test 4—Figure eight at a canter on correct lead, demonstrating a simple change of lead.* The approach to and execution of the figure eight at a canter is exactly the same as for the trot. The rider rides down the middle of the ring at a walk or a slow sitting trot, not a posting trot. As he nears the point of intersection, he collects his horse in preparation for the canter depart on the right lead. After the completion of the circle to the right, he brings his horse back to a walk or a slow sitting trot and, at the intersectional point, he makes a simple change of lead to the left lead and a cantering circle to the left. (Remember that a proper simple change of lead demands several steps of the walk or slow trot.) Just as in the trot work, the rider finishes his eight by a smooth stop on the point of intersection. As in all lateral work, strict attention must be paid to maintaining a regular pace and to the horse's correct bend on the circular tracks. A hurried or sluggish pace or cutting or bulging off the circles should be severely penalized in judging these tests.

*Test 5—Work collectively at a walk, trot, or canter.* What is asked for here is to see whether, after a rider has jumped a course of fences well, he can maintain his over-all riding ability and come back into the ring and ride well on the flat. This conception and judgment is good; we are looking for a good rider, not just a good jumping rider. The rider, at this point in the class, should pay particular attention to his position and use of smooth aids on the flat and, perhaps above all, showmanship.

*Test 6—Pull up and halt between fences except in a combination.* Whenever one must stop a horse after a jump, it is wise to take that jump as collectedly as possible. The faster and "bigger" a jump becomes, the longer it takes to pull up on landing. Another little trick to remember is to angle the fence slightly so that the horse isn't right in line with the next fence. This not only gives the rider more time but also keeps the horse from anticipating the following obstacle. Once the horse has landed, it is up to the rider to make his stop as smooth and as prompt as possible. Both of these factors are terribly important. It is permissible for the rider to use his direct rein, weight, and voice, but only under the most drastic circumstances should a pulley rein be used. This particular rein aid is considered taboo by many equitation judges. Providing the horse will stand, it is advantageous to show the halt for a count of about four seconds.

*Test 7—Jump fences on a figure-eight course.* Occasionally, a judge will call back some of his better contestants and ask them to jump a course in the pattern of a figure eight. Usually this will require a bit more collection and control for the turns through the middle of the ring which, while not particularly difficult for the advanced rider, can be quite challenging for those who are still under fourteen, novice, or limit. The only recommendations that I can make for riding this course would be a slightly slower pace and sharp eye control on the rider's part.

*Test 8—Jump low fences at a walk and trot as well as at a canter.* (The maximum height and spread for a trotting fence is three feet.) The emphasis in this test, of course, is in maintaining the walk or the trot until the horse takes off. In walking a jump, the horse must walk as long as possible before popping the fence. I recommend holding the walk until the very last minute and then using a little cluck to make sure that the horse takes off. This aid, as a rule, eliminates the possibility of a refusal and makes the rider's wishes known to the horse at the right time.

Trotting a fence is psychologically a bit easier for both horse and rider than the walk, due to the added bit of pace. However, to hold the trot until the horse is "off the ground" demands training and practice. Often, one or two cantering steps sneak in and ruin a rider's chances of success in that class. A fairly slow trot, either posting or sitting, usually inhibits horses from cantering the last few strides, and this must be maintained until take-off. I recommend that if a rider does post to the fence, he sink into the saddle a stride out so as to be sure not to jump ahead of his horse. Once the horse feels that added bit of weight strengthen the rider's leg, he's not so apt to "cheat" (put in another short stride) or refuse.

*Test 9—Ride without stirrups.* While to my riders, riding without stirrups isn't really a test as they do it so much at home, I suppose for some people it is an unusual experience. What the judge is looking for, whether over fences or on the flat without irons, is for tightness and independence in both seat and leg. Remember that the leg should be in exactly the same position with the toe held up as when with stirrups. The additional test of dropping and picking up stirrups is a good one in that it is a practical problem all riders face in both riding and jumping: losing one's stirrup and having to regain it. Don't look down to find a stirrup; that is the cardinal sin. Hold your toes up in position and feel around with them until catching the stirrup back; and try not to excite your horse too much while doing so.

*Test 10—Dismount and mount.* While this test is easy to understand for the younger riders, it is not so easy to do if they're mounted on large horses. That is why it is only asked of the older age groups. In order to execute this test properly, read the section on mounting and dismounting in Chapter 1. Make sure after dismounting and before mounting that you go to your horse's head and hold the reins, facing forward toward the middle of the ring. This will give some separation and pause to the two parts of the test.

*Test 11—Half-turn on the forehand.* This test can be asked for by the judge or just used as a basic means of reversing direction in a flat class. In either case, it would be correct at the collected walk or at the halt. The horse should hold a very, very small circle with his forelegs and describe a larger circle with his hind legs, which move about from one direction to the other until the horse has made a 180-degree turn. The bend of the horse in this movement is really immaterial so long as he is not "overbent." It is a leg-yield type of exercise, and therefore the horse should be kept as straight as possible from head to tail while making the turn. The important thing is that the horse yield his haunch from the rider's outside leg, which has gone back a hand; the horse definitely should be prevented from backing up, by the use of both legs of the rider; from popping his shoulder to the inside; and from moving ahead of the pivoted zone.

*Test 12—Execute serpentine at trot and/or canter on correct lead, demonstrating simple or flying changes of lead.* A serpentine is a series of left and right half-circles off the center of an imaginary line. As a rule, this figure commences at the middle of one short side of the ring and finishes at the middle of the other short side, the radius of each half-circle being kept exactly the same from the middle of the ring. In trotting a serpentine, one changes his diagonal whenever crossing the center line and, likewise, when cantering, one makes a simple or flying change when crossing this line. I prefer that the rider start the required gait exactly when reaching the middle of the first short side on the track of the ring. In other words, a rider would move out of line at a walk or a sitting trot and wouldn't move up into a posting trot or canter until reaching the serpentine's starting point. As in all other tests, I very much like a precise finish and feel that a correct halt at the serpentine's termination gives it that added touch of control.

*Test 13—Figure eight at canter on correct lead, demonstrating flying change of lead.* The same approach and pattern is used for this test as in any other figure eight. Unless the judge calls for the first circle to the left, I advise my riders to start to the right, just for the sake of establishing a habitual pattern. After the horse has completed three quarters of his circle to the right, the rider starts preparing for the flying change by straightening his horse with an outside bearing rein and leg. This takes some weight off the left side of the horse, the side that must be lightened in order to take the new lead (left lead). Once this side has been straightened, the rider asks for the new lead by activating his new outside leg (or the right leg). Most horses, until they've learned that this is a signal for the flying change, try to escape the action of the leg by increasing their pace. At all costs this must be prevented by the restraining action of the hands. Another evasion commonly experienced is that of the horse's cutting off the track of the circle with his forehand. This is easily prevented by an outside opening rein. Upon completing the second circle, the rider smoothly halts at the point of intersection and then returns to line.

*Test 14—Change leads down center of ring, demonstrating simple change of lead.* This test is usually called for down the middle of the ring or along the long side. Judges nowadays specify the number of simple changes, which is the way it should be. Let's suppose that the judge requests three simple changes down the center of the ring. Remember this means four leads at the canter. Now the horses are lined up on the long side of the ring and they must peel out one at a time to execute the test. It is best to walk out of line, walk to the end of the ring, and then turn down the middle line. Don't start cantering until you are straight on the line. It's harder that way and shows more control and will impress a judge more than to take the easy way out by picking up your first lead before the turn. If three changes are to be shown, the length of the ring must be divided into four parts. Start cantering as soon as possible after the turn and make the simple changes prompt. There is nothing worse than to run out of ring space and still have another change left to do. A proper simple change of lead should show several steps of walk or slow trot before taking up the new lead. At the end of any line test, a nice straight halt should be in order just to put a frame around the test and show a neat finish.

When doing this test using flying changes, the pattern is exactly the same. The rider establishes a line with his eyes before picking up his first lead and positively holds a line throughout the changes until he halts. At the moment of change, the horse is in a collected canter and straight, and the rider simply brings his outside leg to the rear to request the lead change. One must be careful of the most obvious evasions: the horse ignores the leg and cross-canters behind; he breaks pace to a trot or rushes too fast; he zigzags down the line while making the changes and is very crooked. To do this test properly, one must first have a horse well schooled in flying changes on turns, figure eights, and serpentines.

*Test 15—Change horses or ride strange horse supplied by committee.* Any rider participating in an open equitation event must be prepared to ride someone else's horse. This test can psychologically be the most unnerving of all for those who haven't had much experience on different horses. Almost without exception, the change will take place between riders within the same class, and it is rare indeed to have a third horse brought in by the committee. Naturally, the sharp competitor or coach will be quite familiar with many of the other horses in the ring and will have some clues as to how the horse may best be ridden. Of course it is only "cricket" for the riders and/or teachers to tell each other about their respective animals; anyone not doing this will be blackballed in short order by the people that count. Once the change has been made, it is up to the rider himself to evaluate his horse and how it responds to the different aids, especially the hand and leg. I always have my riders use the same artificial aids, such as sticks and spurs, as the original riders used; very rarely will I add or subtract one of these aids on a change. Sometimes the judges give the contestants a few minutes to feel out their new mounts, which of course makes things easier. On other occasions, though, the contestants go through their test or over their course cold; this isn't as easy and takes experience and feel.

*Test 16—Canter on counter lead.* No more than eight horses may counter canter at one time. The key to this test is to be free from outside interference. No matter how well schooled your horse is, he is apt to change leads when bumped into or cut off. So stay by yourself and watch out for your competitors. I'd say the next consideration would be straightness. It is easy to displace a horse's hindquarters to the outside while riding the long, straight side of the ring; it is not so easy on the short, bent end of the ring. Therefore if the counter lead is called for while you are riding a turn, make your horse as straight as possible before executing the movement. As far as riding a counter canter is concerned, that has been amply covered in the section of this book devoted to work on the flat.

*Test 17—Half-turn on the haunches.* Like the half-turn on the forehand, this test may be called for from the collected walk or from the halt. It is more classically correct, though, to do it from the walk. As a general means of reversing in a flat equitation class, I prefer it above all others for intermediate riders on up. It is a bit too sophisticated for maiden, novice, and the average limit rider. There is nothing more ridiculous than to judge a maiden class and watch a group of little tots try to reverse on the haunch, not knowing what they are doing, and end up doing nothing right! If you can execute the movement correctly, try to show it to the judge in the reverse. We covered the aids fully in this book; now go and put the movement to your advantage on the horse.

*Test 18—Demonstration ride of approximately one minute.* The rider must advise judge beforehand what ride he plans to demonstrate. This is really a wonderful additional test incorporated into the hunter seat equitation section. It allows a rider to show a judge what he knows in an organized manner. The first thing about riding this test is to have it worked out beforehand; there should be no need for improvisation. In fact, a sharp equitation rider will have three or four tests at his disposal at all times. Secondly, the test must be comprehensive but short. In other words, it should combine perhaps six or eight different schooling movements without dragging any one of them out or rushing them artificially together. Thirdly, and this is the name of the game, the test should be the most difficult one that that particular rider and horse are up to and can do well, without making any major mistakes. For instance, a greener entry might only risk a shoulder-in, an extended posting trot, and a short counter canter, while a very schooled pair could safely attempt a two-track, a serpentine on the counter lead, and flying changes down the center line. The point is that, within a very short time, the rider demonstrates his knowledge, ability, and imagination in working with his mount on the flat. Needless to say, this test is limited to riders in the open category.

In sum, the tests from which judges must choose to decide the winners in hunter seat equitation are really just a list of comprehensive exercises that should be done by every rider making every green or young horse at home. There should be nothing "gimmicky" or unnatural about anything asked of an equitation rider, but it should, rather, have a direct and related value to his horse's schooling. Providing the equitation rider is being taught to be a horseman and a trainer, none of these tests should be overly difficult or at all surprising in the show ring. Judges do, on occasion, elaborate and extend these tests so that they override the rules a bit. However, protests are rarely made unless something that is specifically not part of conventional hunter schooling is called for. The one class in which the judges are not confined to the above-mentioned tests is the USET. Since it is more a class preparing the rider for jumper competition, many judges request tests of a more difficult dressage nature such as turns on the haunches, shoulder-in, or even two-tracking. Sometimes over fences in this class, the ride-off course must be ridden with sharp turns simulating a timed jump-off.

All in all, if the rider is given a thorough and comprehensive background in as many phases of equestrian sport as possible and if his exposure to the horse is natural and pointed toward what's known as "horsemastership" in the true sense of the word, he'll find his years in the equitation division the best training ground of all for things to come in the future. For years the American horse show exhibitor has improved and supported this division in the belief that it is a division designed to create good riding. This has indeed been the result. No country in the world can boast of horses and riders schooled to the degree of subtle perfection that ours are. I attribute this not only to our Olympic coach's great system of training but also to a tremendous degree to the background all of these riders have had during their junior years in equitation. These classes speak for themselves as to their value; and they will continue to do so as long as they are maintained as part of the horse showing scene and their standards are never compromised or reduced by horsemen ignorant of the importance of classical equitation.

# PART FIVE

# Some Teaching Suggestions

# 11

# *To the Teacher*

## CONFIDENCE

Teaching is an accepted art; unfortunately, it is often not as accepted in riding as in most other athletic endeavors. There are certain fundamental principles, which, if adhered to, produce better results and a smaller percentage of accidents and accelerate the pupil's progress rate. These principles should be taught in a constructive sequence and with the use of a standard terminology which is concise and simple yet covers a range of equestrian applications. Only through consistent and explicit use of clearly defined terms may a sound, disciplined relationship of communication exist between teacher and rider; this relationship is of paramount importance, establishing a basis of confidence from which progress, ability, and attitude mature.

Confidence is essential in sound teaching. There are several kinds of confidence: the rider's confidence in himself and his ability to control his horse safely; his confidence in his teacher's credentials and knowledge of what is best for his student; and probably the most important confidence of all, the rider's knowing that he isn't being asked to do more than he is physically or mentally capable of. The fear of getting hurt or of having one's ego smashed is destructive to the pupil's progress. In approaching this subject from the instructor's viewpoint, the first question is whether or not the pupil can physically do what is being asked of him. If there are any doubts at all, the situation is too difficult and an accident is likely to take place. In this case the requirements must be modified rather than the rider pushed to questionable limits. Often one hears a small warning "No," a sixth sense, and that instinctive suggestion should be followed. When the instructor realizes that a rider is physically able to approach a difficult problem but is mentally apprehensive, he must work around this fear and convince the pupil tactfully that the situation is surmountable. This depends wholly on each individual's style and is something that cannot be stereotyped. A firm strength of purpose and a sincere positive belief ladled out with sensitive understanding usually make the best recipe. Despotic, frenetic outbursts rarely accomplish much, although on rare occasions they are fun, theatrical, and work wonders!

There are two kinds of fear, physical and mental. When someone is afraid of getting hurt, he is said to have physical fear; when someone is afraid of making a mistake, he has mental fear. With rare exceptions, riders have one or the other, sometimes both in varying degrees. Consequently, the responsibility for understanding each pupil and understanding him in accordance with his particular fear falls solely on the instructor. In general, fear should never be discussed; it is a negative commodity and talking about it really means emphasizing it. In fact, it's axiomatic that if you tell someone to relax, they'll try so hard that they stiffen up.

On occasion one runs into the overconfident rider who is blasé and sloppy. Since genius has been defined as "an infinite capacity for detail," pupils of extraordinary riding teachers should never turn out this way! But such is not the case, even with genius products. So the undermined instructor must again react, teaching the individual accordingly even to the point of shaking his overconfident ego just a bit. Confidence is an elusive quality and must be guarded rigorously. Here today, gone tomorrow, shaken confidence can have disastrous consequences even at Olympic levels. At the root of many sophisticated riding problems, it must be taken into consideration as the cause of any deviation from a normal standard.

## OVERMOUNTING

Perhaps the commonest deterrent to good riding, fast learning, and safe teaching is overmounting, or placing a rider on a horse that he is not able to control easily. I say "easily" because the category of overmounting is not necessarily limited to those riders who are mounted on rogues, runaways, or unbroken horses just off the track. The horse that is just a bit too strong or one who balks once too often is too much for the ordinary rider to learn on.

Overmounting is a tricky business and should be avoided at all costs at the beginner-intermediate levels. Advanced riders should really be able to cope with anything, and so this maxim wouldn't apply to them. Naturally, there are cases and times where horses of suitable temperaments aren't apparently available. In such moments of distress, the horses must be made suitable through use of expedients. Cutting the grain and keeping the horse off hard feed works wonders with temperaments of high mettle. Of course, compensation must be made through added amounts of hay, bran, and soft feed. Turning horses out has miraculous results, relaxing them and providing them with a self-determined amount of exercise. The ones who are lazy and stand around by the paddock fence should be chased around if extra work is warranted. Longeing is a more controlled form of exercise and provides the dual advantage of supplementary training if it is done correctly and efficiently. One of the most thorough means of moderating a horse and bringing him into the range of experienced pupils is to have him worked down by a more experienced horseman. The horse then provides the better rider with a challenge and a schooling opportunity; he is also made pliable and a conveyance for the rider of lesser experience and background.

Not only does this overmounting produce fear and loss of confidence, but it also leads to the rider's total distraction. The novice rider under such conditions is totally absorbed in trying to control a horse that is too much for him. He should, in contrast, be completely free to concentrate solely on himself and his own physical problems. It is impossible for the human mind to concentrate on more than one thing at a time. How then can a student be expected to work on his heels, his eyes, or his hands when he's worried about stopping or being bucked off? Only through self-control will a rider eventually be able to direct his thoughts and energies toward horse control. By carefully avoiding situations of overmounting and by, if anything, undermounting, the rider's progress will be rapid, safe, and happy.

ONE THING AT A TIME

Perhaps the single most important factor attached to rapid progress in learning is for the instructor to teach one thing at a time. In actuality a person's mind can only think of one thing at a time and his concentration should be encouraged in this direction. Habits are quickly and easily established if they are focused upon singly and are given specific emphasis. Dissipation takes place and progress is greatly retarded as soon as the mind becomes cluttered and the body is trying to function in many new directions at once. Although repetition of a single point may seem boring and slow, it is the surest way to success. Therefore the pupil must be inspired to appreciate and enjoy slow, progressive work.

Isolated concentration, difficult for teacher and pupil alike at first, is especially important at the earlier stages of riding although, in principle, it holds through to the most advanced levels of technique. In actual practice, the difficulty lies in one's determination to overlook all the other things that may be wrong for the time being. It is not easy for the instructor to ignore a rider's heel that is up when he has prearranged an exercise dealing with eye control. The point is for the eyes to be the center of concentration until there is some progress noted. The time to correct the heels will come later and be worked on separately. The single greatest obstacle to specific concentration is, of course, the horse itself. That is why it's so important not to overmount, and to consider the horse only as a vehicle and a conveyance for those just learning to ride. Nothing must block the rider's relaxation and confidence by allowing him to focus on more than one thing at a time.

## EXPLANATION—DEMONSTRATION—OBSERVATION

There are basically three ways for the riding teacher to communicate with his pupil—explaining verbally what he wants him to do or not to do, demonstrating right and wrong, and allowing the pupil to observe others. All three assist the rider intellectually in understanding new techniques, which, of course, must be the first step before real feel can be had. I firmly believe that if any one of these means of transmitting information be lacking, the pupil is at a distinct disadvantage.

Let us start with explanation, obviously the number one method for teaching an individual or a group. What is needed from the teacher's point of view and the pupil's, first and foremost, is disciplined attention to what is being said. Now there are several ways to talk to riders depending on the specific situation at the time. If I wish to give short commands or brief critiques concerning known material such as position corrections or the improvement of a schooling movement, I'll discuss the point while the rider continues to work. If, however, I'm going to introduce new material or make a major correction involving lengthy dissertation I'll stop the class or have the class ride in to me. The instructor, to be fair to his pupil, must not only have knowledge of the subject matter at hand, but he must also be able to get this across by means of a better-than-average command of speech. This command should include a good projection, proper diction, and a meaningful sequence of material. A teacher's personality and his credentials usually can be discovered through his voice.

The adage "He can't ride but he can teach" may be true to a certain level but, to my mind, it certainly reaches a point of no return. Given two instructors, one who rides well and one who doesn't, there is no question as to the one I'd choose. There are several very specific reasons to back this up. First, the rider who doesn't (or never did) ride well to the level he is teaching never really experienced through feeling the material he is trying to get across. Without this feeling, he has to be rather limited in his scope of explanation. Secondly, one who doesn't ride very well has an impossible time with our second means of communication—demonstration. There is nothing truer in a riding lesson than the statement "A picture is worth a thousand words." On many an occasion all the conversation in the world between instructor and pupil can't replace one simple little demonstration. Not only should the instructor be able to hop on and show how it should be done, but he should also be proficient enough to copy his pupil's mistake and show him how *not* to do it. A good riding teacher also should at any time be able to get his pupil's horse to do whatever he is asking of it in case its own rider can't. Therefore, while demonstration may not be an absolutely mandatory part of an instructor's credentials to some people, I consider it almost indispensable. Of course there are the exceptions, in which case it's rather a shame, such as a very good teacher who was once a marvelous rider and did experience all the feelings he is trying to get across but who is now physically disabled. In a situation like this, one could overlook, to an extent, the void in demonstrational value and concentrate on getting all he possibly could from valid and, it is hoped, extraordinary explanation.

The observation of others' good and bad points through mediums such as horse shows, the hunting field, and movies is a neglected teaching technique not to be overlooked. To have rider and teacher together analyzing and constructively criticizing what's going on around them certainly can be most educational. Of course, in this instance as in both explanation and demonstration the instructor must be the translator between what his pupil understands and what is being observed at this time. For this reason, I'm very particular as to what my pupils may be exposed to during their early, formative years on horseback; and whenever possible I prefer to accompany them to any public equestrian functions. Uneducated observation can be a very dangerous, damaging thing and many young riders have been seriously retarded by incorrect interpretations. It is up to the instructor to be constantly on the lookout for good and bad examples and to point them out to his protégés at any and every opportunity.

REPETITION

In guaranteeing reward, repetition solidifies confidence, providing of course the repetitive procedures used are conventionally sound. This kind of slow work, practicing basic principles over and over again, precedes any thoughts of advanced, faster aspects of polished riding. To repeat, the basic body control exercises insure the rider a good foundation which must combine security, control, and form. Invisible smooth aids, harmony and balance, along with complete control become certainties in any educated rider's approach to the sport, providing many hours have been spent in the saddle repeating the basic fundamental steps of correct technique.

Oddly enough, though fortunate from the horse's point of view, slow repetitive work carries right on through to the sport's ultimate aspects. Not only does this principle prolong useful physical mechanisms but, what is more important, it also acts as a catalyst in accelerating the process of advancement. By practicing profound, necessary fundamentals at almost the horse and rider's minimum level of capability and potential, strength of habit and relaxation evolve. These latter two ingredients collaborate with talent and rise to the occasion in times of crisis. In preparation and training, rarely does the field hunter gallop full out over rough terrain and trappy obstacles; rather he is jogged slowly and muscled up, popping low fences at random out of this easy pace. What percentage of time is given to the piaffe or passage, the ultimate tests of a Grand Prix dressage horse's collection? Very little indeed compared to the infinite consideration afforded the halt, collected trot, and shoulder-in. The race horse never runs his race nor is the show jumper forced to his peak standard during training. Rather it is the exercising, the build-ups, the momentary glimpses of what lies beneath the surface. The cross rails and the multiple in-and-outs, rather than the entire course of ten fences, teach horses and riders how to jump.

### HABITS

A key word for learning is "habit." At first everything is hard, next it becomes easier, then habitual, and only now does it have a chance to be beautiful. To do something automatically is to do it out of habit. And the primary goal is to get all of the basics out of the way and make them automatic. Then one's concentration is free to work on finesse. Only when the rider's physical instrument has been disciplined enough to be ignored can all of his mental energies be devoted to his horse and his horse's evasions and to how best to correct them in an expedient fashion.

Habits develop through repetition; whether it is correcting position, sequence of aids, or consistent timing, only through regular practice can automatic reaction evolve. Take for example the rider who has difficulty getting his heels down. By standing up in his stirrups in two-point contact and driving weight down into his heels for just five minutes per riding hour, he will develop the correct leg position. On the other hand, he might sporadically work on his heels half an hour but at irregular intervals and never get anywhere. The same sort of thing goes for developing a strong seat, one that is glued into the saddle at the sitting trot and the canter, following the horse's movements with relaxed oscillations of the small of his back. Again, this can be developed through taking a part of every riding hour, perhaps only five or ten minutes and riding without stirrups. It is the daily attendance that counts, not the occasional splurges. Good habits form easily if they are practiced correctly, often, and usually not for extended periods of time all at once. The mind and body can hold a concentration span for just so long before energies must be directed toward something entirely new. For instance, I'll never work on two position exercises in a row but rather do five minutes of body control and then five minutes on a different part of the body's function. In an ideal sequence, this would be followed by the practice or introduction of a new schooling movement. A case in point might be: five minutes of working on leg position in the two-point contact; another five minutes concentrating on how the hands function during increase and decrease of pace at the trot; the last five minutes devoted to teaching the pupil the broken-line schooling exercise, something he has never heard before. This fifteen-minute session has covered a lot of ground. Not only have previously established practices been reviewed and strengthened, but the rider has also been introduced to something new, expanding his knowledge and technique and preventing him from getting bored. There is no one duller or less imaginative than the instructor who drones on about the same thing for half an hour. Very rarely is something integrated into technique during one session. Points are introduced, exercises are repeated and practiced, but it takes extended time spans really to incorporate new material and make it one's own. Profound, proper jumping habits must be dealt with in the same way, yet even more specifically if that is possible.

In short, this is an exercise system of teaching riding. The exercise does the work after the theory has been made clear through explanation, demonstration, and observation. The simple sequence works about like this: explanation of theory, application, correction, demonstration or observation (mental picture), application, correction, repetition (brainwashing) to form good habits. The better the teacher the more the exercise works for him, providing his analysis of the problem and the related corrective exercise are both accurate. Showing, which is actually an exercise in itself, is really just evidence of what the exercise teaching method has developed. As a rule, one should more or less forget the exercises at a show and just concentrate on solving the problems of a particular class, be it on the flat or over jumps. A common teaching error is for the pupil to worry about his homework at a show, rather than just answer the questions to the test. The exercises have supposedly produced automatic riding basics that provide the rider with enough technique to be able and free to concentrate on showing himself and his horse off to their best advantage.

## AVOIDING WASTE MOTION

One of the basic principles of good horsemanship and good teaching is the elimination of what is called "waste motion."

Any aid that could be diminished or any function that could be displaced by a subtler more effective one comes under the category of waste motion or, in other words, overriding. Smoothness and passivity are valuable traits, but they are difficult to achieve after habitual periods, either long or short, of overriding.

We can explain this thesis more clearly by giving specific examples of the overrider's waste motion and the corresponding substitutes. The first and most blatant demonstrations—the kick and the pull—occur when starting and stopping. The uninitiated riders kick and flail their horses into a trot, then pull and haul them back to a stop. Through adherence to the correct aids and their sequence of strength, these overriding manifestations are unnecessary. The point is that the rider must wait and think instead of resorting to crude expedients. His sequence of squeeze cluck-stick (or slap) replaces the kick, is smoother, and is much more efficient. Also, the horse becomes conditioned to respond to a light aid; he knows stronger aids will follow if he doesn't obey. The pull takes more practice as its substitutes depend mostly on weight displacement and a firmly developed seat control. Closing the hand, followed by a sinking of the seat into the saddle, and a straightening of the upper body certainly effect a sounder retardation process than the desperate, pulling technique which is at best crude and at worst useless. In sum, by the introduction of more acute and sharper aids, the horse is more apt to respond quickly and brightly, reducing the rider's task immeasurably. The point is to be able to achieve maximum results with a minimum of effort. Performance is performance, and it must be achieved; the refinement of such and its accomplishment through invisibilities are the criteria. Ducking and throwing the upper body in jumping are examples of obvious violations. Instead of allowing the horse to carry the upper body and close the angles through the thrust of the jump, the rider unnecessarily incorporates much of the work himself. An accurate maxim in riding is "Let the horse do the work."

## FINISHING THE JOB

Discipline and accomplishment go hand in hand, and discipline with a horse means finishing a job. Unlike other achievements, riding deals with another living being, a being which thrives on laxness and habit, be it good or bad. This compounds the problem of discipline and makes it doubly important to finish the job with the horse and rider alike. For something undone sticks in the minds of both animals and humans and becomes more and more a barrier the longer it remains so.

The habit of riding discipline learned from the beginning will never be forgotten. A pupil must become more and more specific in dealing with his own position problems and those concerned with controlling his horse. Each day little goals (of minute but progressive dimensions within the range of an hour's work) should be prearranged, attacked, and accomplished. By attempting too huge a task at once, the most determined rider will become discouraged. For instance, a pupil should make definite progress in eye control for a part of the lesson before going on to, let us say, leg control. He must smoothly stop his horse and make him stand, and only after standing still, go back into a trot. Every little detail should be attended to before student and instructor are satisfied, and this detail should parallel only the advancement made up to that time. Demands of a nature beyond that of the horse's or rider's training must not be expected or considered until the appropriate moment. An excellent point of reference in dealing with discipline and finishing a job is found in the schooling exercises of stopping on a line after a jump. After riding out the line upon landing over a jump, the rider brings his horse to a complete stop at an exact point. Careful attention must be paid to the completion of this job, and deviations of any kind or a slack execution of the exercise must be corrected. Once a job is thoroughly completed, a new one becomes apparent.

## A RIDER'S EMOTION

A rider's emotion should rarely, if ever, enter into his riding sessions; rather, he should rely on intellect, education, and understanding. Emotion colors training too strongly. Being too positive and loving generally leads to undisciplined and sloppy schooling, while a negative, angry approach produces a horse full of tension and fear. Training is best approached in a cool, scientific manner using common sense instead of feelings as guidelines. The rider who constantly thinks ahead and anticipates the outcome of his present attitude toward his horse, rather than his momentary instincts, will find reward in a stable, predictable animal who is not spoiled, disobedient, teasing, or evasive.

An educated understanding of punishment and reward and their varying degrees of application by the rider, should replace a reliance on fickle emotion. Striking examples of wrong behavior are the child who pets his horse upon a refusal at a jump and the butcher who beats up his mount for running out; the stopper more than likely refuses the jump again, having been rewarded for his disobedience, while the horse that ran out, having been beaten, will increase his pace and probably run out again. Both of these reactions to the disobediences were guided by emotion, not reason, doing more harm than good. Tempers as well as gushing sentimentality must be curbed at all times when dealing with horses. This aphorism must be strictly adhered to and enforced by the instructor if progressive training is to occur. The rider who sticks to scientific reaction and consistent, objective reasoning will produce the results we want.

Along with those riders relying on emotion are the face-makers or commenters, those people who consciously or subconsciously wish to communicate their beliefs or feelings of inferiority or superiority to the crowd or instructor and even to themselves when riding alone. This type of rider makes faces and comments on his performance and his horse's performance, usually as a means of excusing his mistakes. Of course this behavior is distracting to the rider; instead of concentrating on remedies, he becomes more unglued and things get worse. As a general rule, focusing on external factors lays ground for disaster. Rider and horse have enough to think about within their own working unit.

In my teaching sessions, the slightest sign of vocal or facial comment is curtailed immediately with no questions asked. Not only is it a matter of common sense reasoning, but, moreover, of discipline. Nothing succeeds like discipline, and anything contrary to regimented work and a serious purposeful approach must be crushed in the embryonic stages. The pupil's slightest peep or raising of an eyebrow are forbidden. Smiling is another anathema of mine during concentrated training, or, worse yet, in the show ring in front of a judge. Numerous times I've heard last-minute orders at the in-gate, "Remember to smile," rather than "Concentrate on pace control" or "Remember your leg position" or perhaps "Work on a little more release in the air." Smiling is very effective off a horse and does wonders in human relations and even sometimes with judges who, surprisingly enough, are often human too. But unfortunately, a radiant smile has nothing to do with precise performance or good riding. So let's eliminate it from purposeful technique.

## LOW JUMPS

Jumping is a very specialized form of riding, almost an entity in itself even though it depends on the balance and control developed on the flat. True, jumping ability can be improved by flat riding, but the latter can never be a substitute for it. Unfortunately, one school of riding evades the very essence of jumping problems and their correction and becomes mesmerized with dressage practice instead. Jumping and dressage are related; and if jumping is not up to standard, it is often due to the wrong kind of dressage or overuse of it. I very definitely believe in a well-broken horse on the flat. It is of paramount importance just from the point of view of obedience. However, if things are going wrong over fences, then the problem must be attacked over fences, and the corrections will probably relate to your flat riding techniques very directly. Only by a rider's concentrating on leg control over the jump will he develop a good jumping leg, no matter how formed and steady his leg is on the flat. Only by jumping and correcting a rusher will he regulate approaching his fences, no matter how much good, basic dressage he has had. The jumps must be attacked directly and consistently. Substitution of emphasis of any kind is, alas, only wishful thinking. Any flat work, no matter how good it is unto itself, must be replaced if it jeopardizes the jumping performance. The actual working or competitive performance must be placed above all else. And the rider who shows the most competence at this hour of decision (not necessarily the classicist, who never performs quite so well over fences) must be examined in light of his flat riding. Basic dressage, with all its dogmas and standards, fine as they are for their own end result, has dangerously become an end in itself as a means of schooling hunters and jumpers. This is unfortunate as many a fine horse and rider have been spoiled for not seeing the forest for the trees.

While conducting this endless practice for horse and rider over fences, it is most important to work over low fences or those not exceeding two feet six inches. For real beginners, a rail on the ground or a cross rail is preferable. Through working on low jumps, the rider can concentrate on form and control. Habits established over low jumps will remain as the jumps are raised, provided drill over modified heights is returned to at regular intervals.

Three goals discussed so far in this chapter—confidence, good habits, and concentration—are only obtainable through jumping modified obstacles. Low fences need no justification in speaking of confidence. Any problems related to confidence should be worked on over negligible heights. Repetition, a mandatory step toward technique, can't be expected over height, just from the point of view of physical stress. The average horse can, on a daily basis, be asked to jump one hundred cross rails per hour, fifty two-foot rails, twenty-five three-foot fences, and about ten three-foot six-inch jumps. Repetition relies on quantity of jumping, not height. The hundred six-inch jumps are what we are after rather than the handful of higher ones. Through this inheritance of confidence and repetition, afforded by infinite numbers of small jumps, habits form quickly and last. The great secret of this kind of work is, of course, the fact that the rider's mind is never apprehensive about getting over the jump. As there is little jump to get over, his mind is free to concentrate on technical matters.

## SUMMARY

A competent teacher in any field is characterized by similar traits revolving around his own technical education, his ability to communicate, and his personality. The mitigation of any one of these three elements undermines the teacher's ability considerably, and to find the consummate combination is rare indeed. Of course, the instructor's previous experience and training are paramount; the greater his own ability and competence, the further and more complete a translation he can offer. A strong, sincere, and sympathetic attitude combined with an affable, attractive mien make for an ideal personality image, one that is destined to evoke the pupil's trust and confidence in his instructor. As a rule, I'm not in favor of a teacher-student relationship becoming too intimate and lax. It's often hard to give orders and to dominate good friends, but this is really up to the individual and the specific case in point. Good communication is important and its positive qualities are strong vocal projection, a comprehensive vocabulary, a sincere interest in explanation and demonstration, and simplicity in approach. Effective voice production, sound grammar, and correct diction are entities unto themselves, and the astute, dedicated instructor who wishes to improve his teaching technique will make every effort to improve his voice in all its details.

# 12

# A Teaching Program

The most important factor of any group teaching project is to stick to a *system*, a system so set, understood, and believed in by those who are teaching and being taught that nothing can really shake its foundations. Don't misunderstand me; I'm not saying that a good new idea or slant on an idea can't replace an old one, but the system itself can't waver. Always remember that almost any method is better than no method at all or a mixture of methods. Naturally, some ways work better than others and any system can be and should be constantly improved by the influx of new thoughts and possibilities.

Unless a riding operation is of very small dimension, the head riding instructor will need one or more teaching assistants. I've had my best luck with assistants who have worked with me beforehand as pupils. They are thoroughly versed in the terminology, ride according to the method, and all in all are comfortable in supporting the ways of their past teacher. Often someone who has not been the most natural or quick starter as a rider ends up being the most capable teacher. This is only natural as he's had to work harder at more problems than the person of easy aptitude and therefore can appreciate and relate to his pupils' problems and faults a bit better.

As I look back over the past, I'd have to say that beginners and intermediates work better with women while the more advanced riders should be with men. Of course this isn't a hard and fast rule, and one exception that I firmly believe in is that most boys should ride with men as soon as possible. Women have a softer, less demanding quality for the novice and timid types, while men will present more challenges and provide the few chills and thrills needed to keep the average boy keen. Each individual's personality must be considered and it's an excellent set-up that can provide a different instructor for different types of people. It's most important that each instructor remember that while he must work within the framework of whatever system is being taught at that particular school and that he must follow a sensible teaching technique, under no circumstances should he lose his individuality. There is nothing worse or more embarrassing than an imitator and a "parrot." Each assistant must constantly renew his inspiration by either working with or watching his chief, but when it comes to putting it across, it must be in his own words and have a freshness of being said for the first time.

There are two great dangers I've found working with subordinates—intimidating and overwhelming them or having them want to replace me. If either of these situations comes to pass, they are no longer useful as assistant instructors and it's time they moved on. Someone too insecure to take the knocks or one who becomes overly competitive can do nothing but create tensions and turmoil. Don't give these types a chance to poison the entire staff and clientele; and that's what usually happens. Out they must go! All in all, though, harmony can be found and usually kept, providing the store is closely watched. And there is nothing more exciting in a riding establishment than to know that different lessons at different levels are all going on at once and that each one is preparing the student for his next step within the system of his choice.

SCHOOL HORSES

Along with instruction and decent facilities, school horses have
much to do with determining the success and rank of the riding
establishment. Without horses qualified to mount every level
of rider, the instructors, no matter how capable, are limited. Of
course, the bigger the operation, the more variety of school
horses must be available. When considering variety I like to categorize my school horses according to their temperaments, with
a view to whether they'll be able to be ridden by beginners, intermediates, or those of advanced riding ability. Those rare
jewels completely reliable for the timid beginner are worth their
weight in gold, as they are hard to find and every school wants
them. Usually I save the really good beginner horse for the beginners and don't waste them and pound them unnecessarily
with more advanced riders. They'll get enough slow work as it is;
and if any bad habits arise I can always get an advanced rider to
straighten them out in a ride or two. This is a policy I always use
with my less advanced horses whenever they need improvement
or correcting. Just put them in a few classes with my better
riders.

An intermediate horse is easier to get hold of. He doesn't have
to have the angelic, slave temperament of the beginner horse
nor the talent desired for advanced work. All he really needs to
be is decent in disposition and adequate in talent. In a large
school there can be quite a range in the horses of this category,
both in temperament and conformation. This is as it should be,
as the biggest group in most schools are intermediate riders and
always will be. Don't forget that soundness in school horses is a
must; they do get worked a lot and, more than likely, can't be
pampered as much as show horses.

Animals for really advanced work usually just happen along
and don't need to be trained for the job. Often they are ex-show

horses or talented intermediate horses with difficult temperaments. By "talented" in this department I'm talking about horses that are capable of easily jumping courses over and beyond three feet six inches. Not only is it unnecessary to have many horses of this caliber in the school, but it is also likely to be unprofitable. First of all, there aren't many people who technically reach the stage where they need to jump big fences, and if they do reach this stage, they'll be headed for the show ring and should have their own horses. I very rarely teach over anything but low fences, a subject which we've already discussed, and when I do work over higher obstacles, it's with a horse and rider in preparation for a horse show. So keep the really advanced work  to private lessons on private horses; it is too risky for your school horse and not necessary.

Many people ask me what I think about ponies for lessons and for children to buy. I have mixed feelings. Ponies usually provide their little riders with two things—a suitable size and a lousy temperament. This temperament thing is what I object to, as it's hard to establish good riding habits while battling the smart little devil for an hour's ride. Of course, falls from little ponies are much less traumatic than from big horses and psychologically this is a big plus. And, let's face it, there are good ponies as well as bad, and a quiet, willing one will be an addition to any riding school. So, if you stumble onto this variety, grab them but don't be surprised to find that you'll have to keep them in line by having them ridden by the better, bigger kids at rather regular intervals.

The most important thing to remember in dealing with school horses, regardless of size or disposition, is that they must be as controllable as possible. There are a few things that must be done at all times with any horse used for this work. First, while he's got to be well cared for, he should never be overfed in relation to the amount of exercise he's getting. I'm very mistrustful of school horses with too much weight. Secondly, these horses have got to get out enough either by turning out, longeing, enough lessons, or just being "topped off" by someone before a lesson. In other words, they should never be above themselves for the beginner or low intermediate. Advanced people can and should be able to cope with almost anything but the beginner and low intermediate should never, never be overmounted. Thirdly, in this same light, it's better to overbit a school horse than take a risk that he can't be stopped. While my really good riders are expected to ride anything in the barn with a snaffle bridle, I'll have many of my school horses in double twisted-wire snaffles or Pelhams. When putting more bit in a horse's mouth I'll usually go in this direction. Double bridles are too sophisticated for the layman; kimberwickes, I've found, get horses throwing their heads; and any other less conventional bridles such as gags could be dangerous. Lastly, I'm a great believer in having all my levels of school horses ridden periodically by good riders. This keeps them ridable and soft, thereby making it much easier for the novice to learn and feel the correct things.

Before finishing on this topic I'd like to forewarn any instructors who are new to running a school about a problem common to us all. And that is the situation that comes about when a pupil becomes wedded to one horse. Unless this person is exceptionally timid, I never allow this to happen. Not only do I find it a particular nuisance to have to work schedules around people and their "pets," but also I'm particularly insistent on having riders, even at an early level, adjust to different horses. This in itself is educational and a confidence builder. So try to see that as a rider develops he rides as many horses as possible. And never let him start determining which horse he is or is not going to ride.

## VARIETY IN PROGRAM

A well-rounded rider is always apt to be better at individual equestrian sport than one who has had a limited, narrow background. The importance of educating oneself to all of riding's different phases cannot be underestimated, and for this reason we are most concerned when running a riding establishment to offer as much variety as possible in the program. Often there is a limit as to how wide a range can be provided, and in such cases as polo, racing, and fox hunting one must go, as a rule, farther afield. For a hunter seat equitation rider to get a chance to do some jumper work, ride test dressage, break a two-year-old, gallop a race horse, or spend a week in a good hunting area is nothing less than stupendous. Any or all of these riding opportunities should be grabbed at a moment's notice.

As far as the average home base operation is concerned, the minimum should allow the pupil the space to work freely on the flat, over stadium jumps in the ring, and over hunter fences both in the ring and on some kind of an outside course. One hopes there is also enough land available with or without fox hunting to get at least a feel of riding naturally forward cross-country. This is terribly important and keeps any horseman loose and free with his horse, which too much ring work is apt to hinder. I try each week to keep as much balance as possible between basic dressage work, hunter schooling, jumper schooling, and going out through the country.

Remember, and never forget, that we are trying to produce horsemen and not just horse show ribbon winners. There is a great difference, and it is interesting to note that the horsemen go on past their junior and equitation years, while the other kind stop riding rather promptly after their eighteenth birthday. A diversified upbringing in riding, as in school, is not only more interesting to the pupil, but also gives him a good chance to feel out where his interests lie with horses for later on. Everyone has his "thing" and this should be encouraged from the start. From the equitation ranks have come great horsemen in many areas. This is the way it should be and the way we want to keep it.

# *Summary*

In conclusion, I'd like to remind the reader of a few things. First of all, the purpose behind being an accomplished equitation rider, or for that matter reading this book, is far from just being able to more easily win an equitation class. I want riders! Horsemen who are technically able to deal with any problem that they may encounter while riding horses. As far as good riding is concerned, I am absolutely convinced that it coincides with smooth riding most of the time. There is lots of inefficiency and waste motion in this field just as there is in any other and it's completely unnecessary. With a scientific approach to equitation, time and money can be saved and horses spared and improved, something all of us want and can get for the little effort it takes to think intelligently.

When a horseman considers his future, he wants to have as many strings to his bow as possible. Limitation and narrow-mindedness are really tragic in the horse world, not only for the professional where they can prove disastrous but also for the keen amateur. Riding jumpers as well as hunters can be twice as much fun as just being up to negotiating an outside course. Dressage work is thrilling and available to many people who reach an age when they shouldn't jump at all. The professional who can teach as well as ride is way ahead of the game. Riding with good form is just as easy for your children to copy as riding with bad form. I could go on and on citing examples of why a good hunter seat equitation foundation is so important. A good high school education is better than a bad one and a bad one is better than none at all.

The satisfactions to me, personally, whether I win or lose when riding myself or when my pupils compete, revolve completely around how I achieved my performance and in the intellectual understanding of the ride. The technical whys and wherefores are all-important, and taking that part of riding away would be very sad indeed. I love the little details, all of them in their most minute proportions. Many a time when I've been showing a hunter or jumper, the unavoidable piece of bad luck has occurred eliminating the chance for a ribbon, yet I've been completely satisfied with the round. On the other hand, many a time I've won a class despite a poor timing move or loss of body control and I'll be down in the dumps for hours. Actually, the relationship between my winnings and my satisfactions in riding and showing is slim indeed. For instance, there is nothing more rewarding to me than to get a horse to the bit, properly flexed on a circle, at a sitting trot. A championship at an "A" horse show means no more.

In short, I hope this material will provide a textbook of sorts for those who are interested in learning to ride a well-rounded seat. Perhaps the practical information will outweigh the idealistic solutions. Or perhaps it will be the other way around? I don't know. There have been many riding manuals that have been valuable and helpful to so many horsemen. If this book can continue to do its share and riding can progress in this decade as it has in the past two, then my effort has been worthwhile. And by the way, many thanks to you readers for sticking it out.